Michael Price & Nick Vandome

Windows 11 for Seniors

in easy steps

for PCs, Laptops and Touch devices

In easy steps is an imprint of In Easy Steps Limited
16 Hamilton Terrace · Holly Walk · Leamington Spa
Warwickshire · United Kingdom · CV32 4LY
www.ineasysteps.com

Notice of Liability
Every effort has been made to ensure that this book
contains accurate and current information. However, In
Easy Steps Limited and the author shall not be liable for
any loss or damage suffered by readers as a result of
any information contained herein.

Trademarks
Microsoft® and Windows® are registered trademarks
of Microsoft Corporation. All other trademarks
are acknowledged as belonging to their respective
companies.

In Easy Steps Limited supports The Forest Stewardship
Council (FSC), the leading international forest
certification organization. All our titles that are printed
on Greenpeace approved FSC certified paper carry the
FSC logo.

MIX
Paper from
responsible sources
FSC® C020837

Printed and bound in the United Kingdom

ISBN 978-1-84078-933-1

Contents

Searching and organizing   93

Classic applications   117

Universal apps   127

8 Email and more 145

9 Internet 165

13 Security and maintenance 219

1 Getting Windows 11

This chapter explains how Windows 11 has evolved, identifies the new features, and shows what's needed to upgrade your existing computer. It also details how to create a Microsoft account.

Windows 11

Windows 11 is the latest release of Microsoft Windows, the operating system for personal computers. There has been a long list of Windows releases, including:

- 1995   Windows 95
- 1998   Windows 98
- 2000   Windows Me
- 2001   Windows XP
- 2003   Windows XP MCE
- 2007   Windows Vista
- 2009   Windows 7
- 2012   Windows 8
- 2013   Windows 8.1
- 2015   Windows 10
- 2021   Windows 11

When you buy a new computer, it is usually shipped with the latest available release of Windows. This takes advantage of the hardware features generally available at the time. Each year sees new and more powerful features being incorporated into the latest computers. In line with this, the requirements for Microsoft Windows have increased steadily. For example, the minimum and recommended amounts of system memory have increased from 4 megabytes (MB)-8MB in Windows 95, to 1 gigabyte (GB)-4GB in Windows 11. There's a similar progression in terms of the processor power, the video graphics facilities and the hard disk storage requirement.

This means that your computer may need upgrading or extending in order to use a later release of Windows, especially if you want to take advantage of new capabilities such as touch gestures. To take full advantage of new features, you may need a new computer; for example, a tablet PC.

Each release enhances existing features and adds new facilities. Thus, the latest Windows 11 is able to support all the functions of Windows 10 and prior releases, along with enhancements, plus its own unique new features. These allow you to carry out tasks that might not have been supported with previous releases of the operating system.

Don't forget

Within each Microsoft Windows release there are several editions catering for different types of users, such as Home, Pro and Enterprise.

Which release is installed?

To check which release of Windows is currently installed on your system, you can look at the **System** panel, which is located in the **Settings** app. This can be accessed in different ways.

- Press the **WinKey** + **Pause** key in any version of Windows to display the **System** panel.

- Click on the **Settings** app on the Taskbar at the bottom of the screen and click on the **System** option in the left-hand panel and then the **About** option.

- Right-click on the **Start** button on the Taskbar and click on the **System** option.

WinKey is another name for the **Windows logo** key. The **Pause** key is labeled Pause/Break.

For all three methods, the operating system details will be shown (along with user, memory and processor information). This includes the version of Windows being used, listed under **Windows specifications** > **Version**.

← Settings — □ ✕

Nick Vandome
nickvandome@gmail.com

Find a setting 🔍

| System | **System** › **About** |

Bluetooth & devices

Network & internet

Personalization

Apps

Accounts

Time & language

Gaming

Accessibility

Privacy & security

Windows Update

Nicklaptop
Aspire V3-531 — Rename this PC

ⓘ Device specifications — Copy ⌃

Device name	Nicklaptop
Processor	Intel(R) Pentium(R) CPU 2020M @ 2.40GHz 2.40 GHz
Installed RAM	8.00 GB (7.82 GB usable)
Device ID	DC546036-4A4D-40DA-B9BF-F9EBFD0A3AF5
Product ID	00330-80000-00000-AA860
System type	64-bit operating system, x64-based processor
Pen and touch	No pen or touch input is available for this display

Related links   Domain or workgroup   System protection   Advanced system settings

▦ Windows specifications — Copy ⌃

Edition	Windows 11 Pro Insider Preview
Version	22H2
Installed on	6/1/2022
OS build	25126.1000
Experience	Windows Feature Experience Pack 1000.25126.1000.0

Microsoft Services Agreement
Microsoft Software License Terms

The next three pages cover some of the new features in Windows 11.

The color of the **Start** menu and the Taskbar below it can be set to **Light** or **Dark**. To do this, select **Settings** > **Personalization** > **Colors** and select **Light** or **Dark** in the **Choose your mode** section. The color of the Start menu and the Taskbar are a matter of personal taste. The majority of the examples in the book use the **Light** option.

Features of Windows 11

Windows 11 includes a number of updates and bug fixes and offers various new features, including the following:

Redesigned interface
Windows 11 features a clean design with rounded corners and pastel shades, similar to the interface for Mac computers.

Updated Start button and Start menu
Two of the most important elements of Windows have been redesigned in Windows 11: the **Start button**, which has always been in the bottom left-hand corner, now takes up a more central position, with the Taskbar centered on the screen rather than stretching all the way across it; and the **Start menu** has been completely redesigned to make it easier to find apps and files.

For anyone who likes the **Start** button in its traditional location in the bottom left-hand corner of the screen, it can still be placed here – see page 31 for details.

...cont'd

Integrated Android apps

Android apps can be accessed via the Amazon Appstore, which is available from within the updated Microsoft Store.

Search

Search has moved from the Taskbar where it appeared in Windows 10, and is now found at the top of the **Start** menu panel. However, there is still a Search icon on the Taskbar.

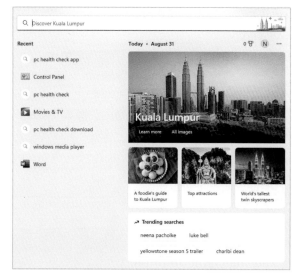

Widgets

You can access widgets directly from the Taskbar and personalize them to see whatever you'd like.

Don't forget

If the Taskbar and the **Start** button are in the default centered position, the **Widgets** icon appears at the far left-hand side of the Taskbar.

...cont'd

Microsoft Teams and the Chat app

The **Teams** option, and the independent **Chat** app, appears on the Windows 11 Taskbar, making it easier to access. This means you can now access Teams from Windows, Mac, Android or iOS.

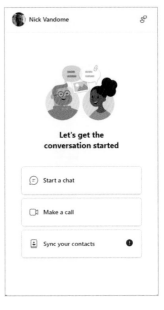

The **Chat** function is incorporated into the **Microsoft Teams** app, and it also appears as its own app, accessed from this icon on the Taskbar.

Snap Layouts

Some previous versions of Windows, including Windows 10, had options for displaying and managing multiple apps within a single screen, known as **Snap Layouts**. This has been refined in Windows 11 so that the layouts can be accessed from the control buttons at the top of each app, based on pre-designed templates.

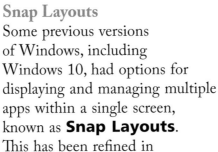

Xbox gaming

Windows 11 has features as found in Xbox consoles, like Auto HDR and DirectStorage, to improve gaming on your Windows PC.

Virtual desktop support

Windows 11 allows you to set up virtual desktops so that you can toggle between desktops for personal, work, school or gaming use. Each virtual desktop can have its own wallpaper.

What's needed

The minimum configuration recommended by Microsoft to install and run Windows 11 is as follows:

- **Processor**   64-bit, 1GHz or faster.

- **System memory**   4GB.

- **System firmware** Unified Extensible Firmware Interface (UEFI)- and Secure Boot-capable.

- **Security**   Trusted Platform Module (TPM) 2.0 encryption device.

- **Graphics card**   DirectX 12 devices or later with Windows Display Driver Model (WDDM) 2.0 driver.

- **Hard disk drive**   64GB (or larger).

- **Optical drive**   DVD/CD (for installation purposes).

- **Display**   High-definition (720p), 9" diagonal or greater, with 8 bits per color channel.

There may be additional requirements for some features; for example:

- Internet access for online services and features such as Windows Update.

- Five-point touch hardware for touch functions.

- A network and multiple PCs running Windows 11 for file and printer sharing.

- An optical drive with rewriter function for DVD/CD authoring and backup function.

- Audio output (headphones or speakers) for music and sound in the Media Player.

If you are not able to upgrade your existing PC to Windows 11 and are not ready to switch to a new device, Windows 10 will continue to be supported until October 14, 2025.

The terms "32-bit" and "64-bit" relate to the way the processor handles memory. You'll also see the terms "x86" and "x64" used for 32-bit and 64-bit respectively.

The product functions and the graphics capabilities may vary depending on the system configuration.

PC Health Check

If you have an older PC, you can check whether your device is capable of running Windows 11 using **PC Health Check**.

Don't forget

If you don't find the app on your system, you can go to https://aka.ms/ GetPCHealthCheckApp to download and run the **PC Health Check** setup app to install the app.

 1 Click the **Start** button and type "pc health check"

```
Q  pc health Check

All   Apps   Documents   Web   More ˅            7575 ⚑  M  ···

Best match

    PC Health Check
    App

Search the web                              PC Health Check
                                                   App
    ⌕ pc he - See web results   >
```

2 Select the **PC Health Check** app when it appears

```
PC Health Check                                    —  ☐  ✕

PC health at a glance

                        Introducing Windows 11
                        Let's check if this PC meets the system requirements.
                        If it does, you can get the free upgrade when it's available.
DESKTOP-F9078UJ         Check now

8 GB RAM
512 GB SSD              ⚙ Backup & sync                    ✓ Backing up  ˄
Less than 1 year old
                           You're signed in and backing up
Rename your PC             Keep your preferences in sync across devices,
                          and set up OneDrive to sync your files, too.     Signed in

                        ⚙ Remember my preferences            ⚪ On

                        ◯ OneDrive folder syncing             Manage

                        ↻ Windows Update        Last checked: Saturday 10:01 AM  ˅

ⓘ About                 ☐ Storage capacity                   35% full  ˅

Learn more about your
device in the Dell      ⊘ Startup time                       See details ˅
SupportAssist App

Related links              Tips on PC health        More on Windows 11
```

Hot tip

PC Health Check will display the memory, disk drive size and the PC age, and provides the facility to rename your PC.

 3 Click **Check now** to see if the PC meets the requirements for Windows 11

If the system meets the requirements, you get a message confirming that the device supports Windows 11.

The requirements may be updated as Microsoft adds more processors to the list of those supported by Windows 11.

However, if your device doesn't meet the current requirements, you will given a list of areas that gave rise to the problem.

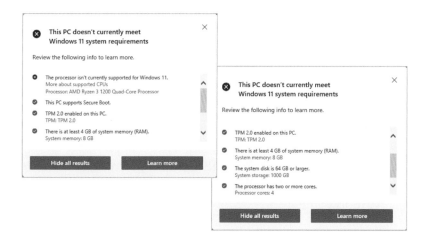

In either case, you can click the **See all results** button, and then be able to scroll through the list of requirements.

Each requirement is shown along with the actual value for the device. For example, it says at least 4GB system memory is needed, while there is actually 8GB installed.

In this example, all the requirements are satisfied except for the installed processor, which isn't currently supported.

A Microsoft account is needed to synchronize settings and access the Microsoft Store to download apps and updates. You can create a Microsoft account from **Accounts** in the **Settings** app (see Chapter 4).

When there is already a PC associated with the Microsoft account, you can choose to copy Windows apps and settings from that PC, or set up your system as a new PC.

Installing Windows

Windows 11 is an online service, rather than just a stand-alone operating system. This means that by default, Windows 11 is obtained and downloaded online, with subsequent updates and upgrades also provided online on a regular basis.

The main ways of installing Windows 11 are:

- **Windows Update** – Replace an older version of Windows, retaining the installed applications and settings. This can be done through the **Settings** app (select **Windows Update** and click on the **Check for updates** button).

- **Microsoft website** – Visit the software download page on the Microsoft website (**microsoft.com/en-us/software-download/windows11**) to use the **Windows 11 Installation Assistant** to download Windows 11.

- **Pre-installed** – Buy a new PC or laptop with Windows 11 already installed.

- Microsoft has now made a DVD available to install Windows 11 directly, rather than via additional updates.

Some of the steps that the installation will go through are:

- **Personalize**. These are settings that will be applied to your version of Windows 11. These settings can also be selected within the **Settings** app once Windows 11 has been installed.

- **Settings**. You can choose to have express settings applied, or customize them.

- **Microsoft account**. You can set up a Microsoft account during installation, or once you have started Windows 11.

- **Privacy**. Certain privacy settings can be applied during the setup process for Windows 11.

Keyboard shortcuts

As you become more confident using Windows 11, you may want to access certain items more quickly. There are a range of keyboard shortcuts that can be used to access some of the items you use most frequently.

The majority of shortcuts are accessed together with the **WinKey** (Windows key) on the keyboard.

To use the keyboard shortcuts, press:

- **WinKey** to access the Start menu at any time.

- **WinKey** + **L** to lock the computer and display the Lock screen.

- **WinKey** + **I** to access the Settings app.

- **WinKey** + **K** to connect new devices.

- **WinKey** + **Q** to access the Search window.

- **WinKey** + **D** to access the desktop.

- **WinKey** + **M** to access the desktop with the active window minimized.

- **WinKey** + **E** to access File Explorer, displaying the Home folder.

- **WinKey** + **T** to display thumbnails on the desktop Taskbar.

- **WinKey** + **U** to access the Accessibility options in the Settings app.

- **WinKey** + **X** to access the Power User menu, which gives you quick access to items including the desktop and File Explorer.

- **Alt** + **F4** to close a Windows 11 app, or close Windows 11 from the desktop.

- **Ctrl** + **Shift** + **Esc** to access Task Manager.

Don't forget

You can change the image that is displayed on the Lock screen, and even provide your own image (see page 69 for details).

Using a Microsoft account

A Microsoft account is required to get the most out of Windows 11 and many of its functions. This is a registration system (which can be set up with most email addresses and a password) that provides access to a number of services via the Windows 11 apps. These include:

Beware

Without a Microsoft account you will not be able to access the full functionality of the apps listed here.

- **Mail**. This is the Windows 11 email app that can be used to access and manage your different email accounts.

- **Teams**. This is the collaboration and communication app.

- **People**. This is the address book app, accessed from the Mail app (above).

- **Calendar**. This is the calendar and organizer app.

- **Microsoft Store**. This is the online store for previewing and downloading additional apps.

- **OneDrive**. This is the online backup and sharing service.

Creating a Microsoft account

It is free to create a Microsoft account. This can be done with an email address and, together with a password, provides a unique identifier for logging in to your Microsoft account and the related apps. There are several ways in which you can create and set up a Microsoft account:

- During the initial setup process when you install Windows 11. You will be asked if you want to create a Microsoft account at this point. If you do not, you can always do so at a later time.

- When you first open an app that requires access to a Microsoft account. When you do this, you will be prompted to create a new account.

- From the **Accounts** section of the **Settings** app (see page 65).

...cont'd

Whichever way you use to create a Microsoft account, the process is similar.

1 When you are first prompted to sign in with a Microsoft account you can enter your account details, if you have one, or

> ×
> ■■ Microsoft
> **Sign in**
> Email, phone, or Skype
> No account? Create one!
> Sign in with Windows Hello or a security key ⑦
> Next
> 🔍 Sign-in options

2 Click on the **No account? Create one!** link

> No account? Create one!

Hot tip

Microsoft account details can also be used as your sign-in for Windows 11.

21

3 Enter your name, an email address and a password (on the next screen) for your Microsoft account

> ■■ Microsoft
> **Create account**
> amy_marie@gmail.com   ×
> Use a phone number instead
> Get a new email address
> Back   Next

4 Click on the **Next** button to move through the registration process

> Next

5 A verification code is required to finish setting up the Microsoft account. This will be sent to the email address entered in Step 3. Click on the **Next** button to complete the Microsoft account setup

> ■■ Microsoft
> ← amy_marie@gmail.com
> **Verify email**
> Enter the code we sent to **amy_marie@gmail.com**. If you didn't get the email, check your junk folder or try again.
> Enter code
> ☑ I would like information, tips, and offers about Microsoft products and services.
> Choosing **Next** means that you agree to the Privacy Statement and Microsoft Services Agreement.
> Next

Closing Windows 11

When you finish working with Windows, you'll want to shut down or sign out. Here are three ways to do this:

Hot tip

If supported by your hardware, you are offered the option to put the PC to sleep. You'd use **Sleep** when you're going to be away from your PC for a while. It uses very little power, and when you return and touch the screen or move the mouse, the PC starts up quickly, and you're back to where you left off.

Apps and Features
Power Options
Event Viewer
Device Manager
Network Connections
Disk Management
Computer Management
Windows Terminal
Windows Terminal (Admin)
Task Manager
Settings
File Explorer
Search
Run
Shut down or sign out >
Desktop

Sign out
Sleep
Shut down
Restart

1 Right-click the **Start** button (or press **WinKey + X**) and select **Shut down or sign out**, then choose the particular option that you require; e.g.

Sign out
Sleep
Shut down
Restart

2 On the Start menu, click the **Power** button to select **Sleep** (if offered), **Shut down** or **Restart**

Sleep
Shut down
Restart

Michael Price

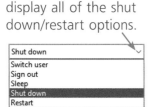

Don't forget

In Step 3, click the **Down** arrow to display all of the shut down/restart options.

Shut down
Switch user
Sign out
Sleep
Shut down
Restart

3 From the desktop you can also press **Alt + F4** to display the **Shut down** option

Shut Down Windows

What do you want the computer to do?

Shut down

Closes all apps and turns off the PC.

OK   Cancel   Help

2 Windows 11 interface

Windows 11 offers a new user interface with a clean design featuring pastel shades and a centralized Start button and Start menu. This chapter shows how to get started with the latest version of Windows, including details of using apps with Windows 11.

Starting Windows 11

Switch on your computer to start up the operating system. The stages are as follows:

 A simple Windows logo is displayed, with a rotating cursor to show that the system is being loaded

 After a while, the **Lock** screen is displayed

Hot tip

The start-up time depends on the configuration of your computer and how it was previously closed down, but usually it is less than a minute.

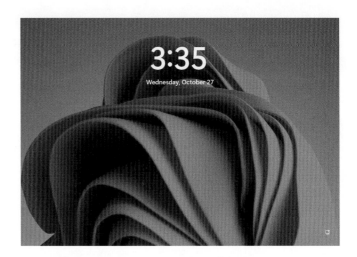

3:35
Wednesday, October 27

3 Press any key, click a mouse button, or swipe up on a touchscreen monitor to display the user **Sign in** screen

Michael Price

Password →

I forgot my password

Sign-in options

24

4 Type the password and click the arrow (or press the **Enter** key)

Don't forget

If there are multiple user accounts, you may need to select the required account before signing in.

5 A **Welcome** message is displayed while the user account settings are being applied

Beware

An error message is displayed when you mistype the password.

That password is incorrect.

6 The Windows 11 desktop screen is displayed, showing the image associated with your account

Beware

The desktop screen features the Taskbar at the bottom and centered.

PIN code sign-in

If you specified a personal identification number (PIN) code during install or added one later using **Settings** > **Accounts** (see page 86), you can sign in using this.

The sign-in options will include, from left to right: **Picture**; **Password**; and **PIN**.

 The **Sign in** screen will request the PIN code

Windows remembers the last sign-in option used, and presents that option the next time you sign in with that account.

2 To sign in with the PIN code, just type the four digits – there is no arrow to click and no need to press **Enter**

3 To revert to the password, select **Sign-in options** and click the **Password** button

 After sign-in, whichever technique was used, the Windows 11 desktop will be displayed

Multiple user accounts

1 If you want a different account from the one suggested, click the required account in the list

2 Enter the password to sign in to the selected account

3 A **Welcome** message is displayed while the account details are being loaded

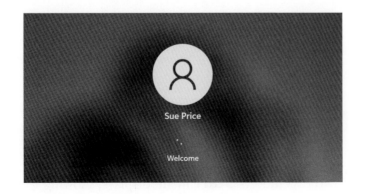

4 Finally, the desktop screen will be displayed

If there is more than one user account, the **Sign in** screen will display the last used account, along with a list of available accounts. (See page 78 for how to add other users.)

The account you choose could be a Local account or a Microsoft account. Only the latter can be used to download content from the Microsoft Store. A Local account is created with a username (which is not an email address) and password, and it grants access only to the device it is created on.

27

Start button and Start menu

The **Start** button and the Start menu have been updated in Windows 11.

Windows systems start up on the desktop, and you can display the Start menu using the **WinKey** or the **Start** button.

This Start menu is from a fresh install of Windows. You'd expect more entries for an active system that was upgraded to Windows 11. Also, entries get added as you use the system.

When you start Windows, you can see the apps and programs that are provided. These vary depending on the edition of Windows installed.

Michael Price

1 From the **Lock** screen, sign in using your PIN code or password to display the desktop

2 On the desktop, click the **Start** button on the left of the Taskbar icons (or press or tap the **WinKey**)

3 The Windows **Start** menu displays, showing the **Search bar**, **Pinned** apps, **Recommended** files and a button for the **All apps** list

4 Click the **All apps** button in Step 3 on the previous page to see your **Most used** apps and an alphabetical list of all your apps

All apps >

Don't
forget

Entries with a folder icon expand when you click them and contain groups of items. For example:

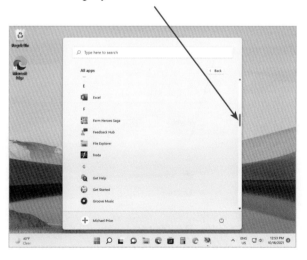

	Windows Ease of Access
	Magnifier
	Narrator
	On-Screen Keyboard
	Windows Speech Recognition
	Windows Security

5 Move the mouse pointer to the right of the Start menu to display the scroll bar

Hot tip

At the bottom of the Start menu is the active user account. Click this to change its settings or to select a different user account.

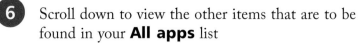

👤	Change account settings
🔒	Lock
➦	Sign out
👤	Sue Price
➕	Michael Price

6 Scroll down to view the other items that are to be found in your **All apps** list

29

...cont'd

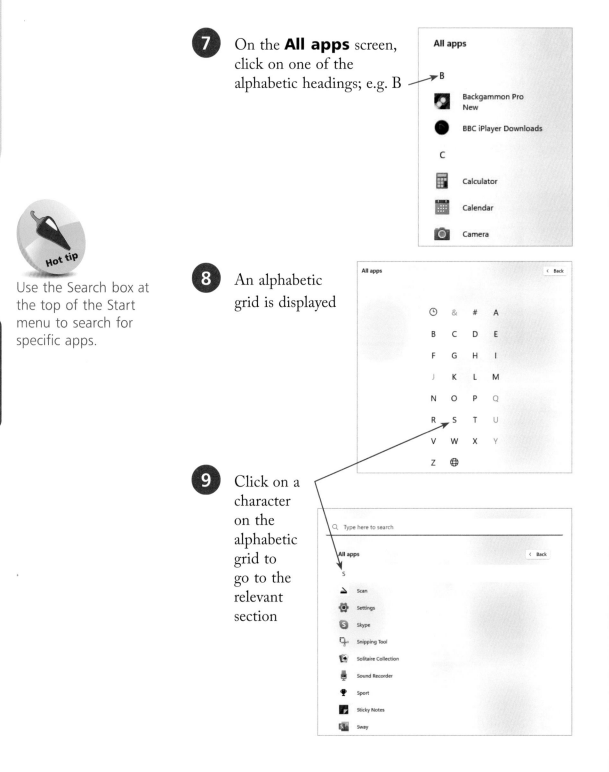

7 On the **All apps** screen, click on one of the alphabetic headings; e.g. B

All apps

B

Backgammon Pro
New

BBC iPlayer Downloads

C

Calculator

Calendar

Camera

8 An alphabetic grid is displayed

All apps   < Back

🕐   &   #   A

B   C   D   E

F   G   H   I

J   K   L   M

N   O   P   Q

R   S   T   U

V   W   X   Y

Z   ⊕

9 Click on a character on the alphabetic grid to go to the relevant section

Q Type here to search

All apps   < Back

S

Scan

Settings

Skype

Snipping Tool

Solitaire Collection

Sound Recorder

Sport

Sticky Notes

Sway

Repositioning the Start button

Although the **Start** button has moved into a more central position, along with the Taskbar, it is still possible to restore it to the left-hand corner if desired. This is done by moving the whole of the Taskbar to the left. To do this:

1 Click on the **Settings** app on the Taskbar or the **Start** menu

Settings

2 Click on the **Personalization** tab

Personalization

3 Click on the **Taskbar** option

Taskbar
Taskbar behaviors, system pins

4 Click on the **Taskbar behaviors** option

Taskbar behaviors
Taskbar alignment, badging, automatically hide, and multiple displays

5 Click here in the **Taskbar alignment** panel to select options for how the Taskbar is aligned

Taskbar behaviors
Taskbar alignment, badging, automatically hide, and multiple displays

Taskbar alignment   Center

6 Click on the **Left** option to align the Taskbar to the left-hand side, situating the **Start** button in the left-hand corner

Left

Center

Repositioning the **Start** button is a new feature in Windows 11.

Don't forget

In Step 6, all of the icons on the Taskbar are aligned to the left, in addition to the **Start** button.

Power User menu

There's a menu of useful shortcuts associated with the **Start** button (on the left of the Taskbar icons).

The **Power User** menu is also known as the **WinX** menu, referencing the keyboard shortcut.

 Right-click the **Start** button to display the **Power User** menu

 Alternatively, press **WinKey** + **X** to display that same menu

This allows you to access a set of functions that are often needed by the more advanced user, which include the System panel, Device Manager, Disk Management, Windows Terminal, Task Manager, Settings, and Run.

Select the **Shut down or sign out** option, and you can choose to sign out, sleep, shut down or restart your system.

Make sure that it's the **Start** button that you right-click, or you'll get the right-click action associated with the alternative area you click. On the desktop, for example, you would get the Screen menu with View, Sort by, Refresh, etc.

It is easy to click or touch the wrong spot and get an unexpected result, especially on a touchscreen system.

Right-click the Taskbar and you get the option to open the **Taskbar settings**.

This opens **Settings** at the **Personalization** option, with Taskbar selected, so you can adjust the Taskbar properties.

 Show or hide the Taskbar buttons:
Search
Task view
Widgets
Chat

Scroll down to reveal a list of Taskbar corner icons and, for each icon, choose **On** to show the icon or **Off** to hide it

Click the **Up** arrow (^) on the Taskbar to reveal the contents of the Taskbar corner overflow.

Scroll on down to show the Taskbar corner overflow

Choose which icons may appear in the Taskbar corner

Scroll on down to the **Taskbar behaviors** section, where you can select the setting for Taskbar alignment or choose the **Automatically hide the Taskbar** option, when you move the mouse pointer away from the Taskbar area.

You can also choose **Show badges (unread messages counter) on taskbar apps**, and **Show recent searches when I hover over the search icon**.

33

An icon appears to the right of the date and time on the Taskbar, to indicate the number of new notifications to be viewed.

Desktop layout

Both tablet and standard PCs start with the desktop screen. This is similar to the display from earlier versions of Windows, with desktop icons, and the Taskbar with **Start** button, shortcuts and active apps, Quick settings and the date and time. Here, you see a Classic app and two Universal apps running in windows on the desktop.

Desktop icon   Universal apps   Classic app   Background

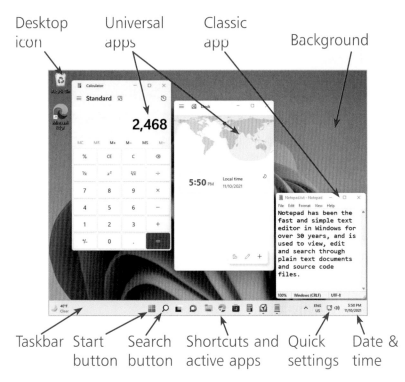

Taskbar   Start button   Search button   Shortcuts and active apps   Quick settings   Date & time

Left-click the date & time (or press **WinKey** + **N**) to display a flyout bar on the right of the screen. This displays the **Notifications area**, beneath which is the entry for the calendar.

Left-click the **Up** or **Down** arrows to expand or contract the calendar. It shows the current day and date. When expanded, it will show the current month with the current day selected.

When you left-click the **Network** icon or the **Volume** icon (or press **WinKey** + **A**), you will display the **Quick settings** flyout.

...cont'd

Click the **Start button** to display the **Start menu**: a merger of the features of the Start menu and the Start screen from previous versions of Windows.

Pinned apps   Recommended apps   All apps button

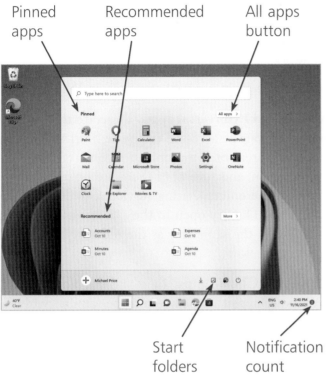

Start folders   Notification count

To close the Start menu and redisplay the desktop, click the **Start** button, click anywhere on the screen outside the Start menu, or press the **WinKey**.

Click the **More >** button to display a longer list of recommended apps.

1   Scroll the **All apps** list to see the full set of apps on your system

2   Right-click the **File Explorer** icon on the Taskbar to get links to the desktop and to specific parts of the file system, including **Downloads**, **Documents** and **Pictures**, and also to list your frequently accessed files

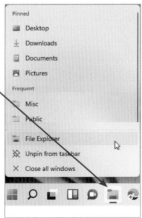

To close the folder list, left-click anywhere on the screen away from the folder list itself.

35

Windows 11 Universal apps are so named because they can be used on a range of devices running Windows 11, including tablets and touchscreen computers. They are generally newer apps than the older Windows Classic apps. They will be referred to as Universal apps throughout the book, unless otherwise stated.

Don't forget

In Windows 11, all apps open directly on the desktop and their operation is more consistent, regardless of the type of app.

Using apps with Windows 11

The word "app" is now firmly established as a generic term for computer programs on a range of devices. Originally, apps were items that were downloaded to smartphones and tablet computers. However, the terminology has now been expanded to cover any computer program. So, in Windows 11 most programs are referred to as "apps", although some legacy ones may still be referred to as "programs".

There are three main types of apps within Windows 11:

- **Windows 11 Universal apps**. These are the built-in apps that can be accessed from the Start menu. They cover the areas of communication, entertainment and information, and several of them are linked together through the online sharing service, OneDrive. In Windows 11, they open in their own window on the desktop, in the same way as the older-style Windows apps (see below).

- **Windows Classic apps**. These are the older-style Windows apps that people may be familiar with from previous versions of Windows. These open in the desktop environment.

- **Microsoft Store apps**. These are apps that can be downloaded from the online Microsoft Store, and cover a wide range of subjects and functionality. Some Microsoft Store apps are free, while others have to be paid for.

...cont'd

Windows 11 Universal apps
Windows 11 apps are accessed from the icons on the Start menu. Click on an icon to open the relevant app.

Windows Classic apps
Windows Classic apps are generally the ones that appeared as default with previous versions of Windows, and would have been accessed from the **Start** button.

For Android users on smartphones and tablets, **Android apps** can also now be downloaded with Windows 11, which is a new feature.

Windows Classic apps can be accessed from the Start menu by using the alphabetic list, or searched for via the Taskbar Search box. Windows Classic apps have the traditional Windows look and functionality, and they also open on the desktop.

Microsoft Store apps
Microsoft Store apps are accessed and downloaded from the online Microsoft Store. Apps can be browsed and searched for in the Store, and when they are

downloaded they are added to the **All apps** alphabetic list on the Start menu.

The Microsoft Store is accessed by clicking on the **Microsoft Store** tile on the Start menu or on the Taskbar.

Hot tip

With a Windows 11 touchscreen or tablet, tap the tile to start the app. With the keyboard, navigate to the required tile using the arrow keys and then press **Enter**.

Don't forget

You may be prompted to enter information; for example, to specify the temperature scale for the **Weather** app to use.

Opening an app

Universal and Classic apps may be found as icons on the Taskbar and the **Pinned** section of the Start menu, or alphabetically in the **All apps** list.

1 To open an app, move the mouse pointer over one of the entries for the desired app – **Weather**, for example – and left-click to open it

2 The app opens full-screen or windowed, depending on how it was last loaded, with weather details for the default location

3 Switch back to the **Start** menu to choose another app – **Maps**, for example

4 The app opens, again either full-screen or windowed, overlaying the previous app

5 Load a couple more apps, such as Paint and **Microsoft Edge**, to give a total of four apps

...cont'd

Individual apps may be shown full-screen or windowed. You can follow the same procedures in either case.

When you have several apps running, you can show all active apps and choose one to work with next.

1 Click the **Task View** button (or press **WinKey + Tab**) to show all the apps, and click on one

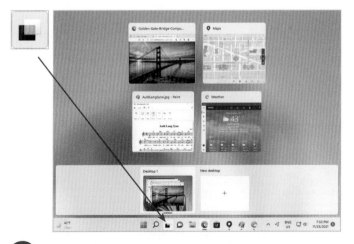

You can organize your apps on several desktops, keeping related apps together – for example, a work desktop and a gaming desktop. See pages 47-48 to set up a new desktop.

2 Alternatively, hold down the **Alt** key and tap the **Tab** key until the app you want is selected, then release **Alt**

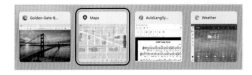

Arranging app windows

You can arrange your active apps manually, by dragging them into the required positions.

Here, we have four apps open, the most that are usually set to share the screen and be viewed at the same time.

1 Start with several apps open, as windows on the desktop, or as full-screen

2 Click the **Title bar** on one app and drag it to the side of the screen, and release the mouse button when a frame appears showing the new location

You can select an app and press **WinKey + Left** arrow or **WinKey + Right** arrow to split the screen, then select a second app for the other half.

40

3 The other apps are displayed in Task View style on the other half of the screen. Select an app to be displayed in that half

Click and drag the edges of a windowed app to resize it on the screen.

With two apps displayed side by side, click and drag the edge between them to widen one window and narrow the other.

41

4 To arrange four apps on the screen, click on the **Title bar** of each app in turn and drag it to a corner

Hot tip

You can position apps in corners using the keyboard. Press **WinKey** + **Left** arrow then **Up** arrow for the upper-left corner. For the other corners, use the (**Right**, **Up**), (**Left**, **Down**) and (**Right**, **Down**) combinations.

If you have a dual-monitor system, you can have sets of two or more apps displayed on each monitor.

Snap Layouts is a new feature in Windows 11.

You can also press the **WinKey** + **Z** key combination to display the Snap Layouts feature.

If you have set **Portrait** rather than **Landscape**, you'll be offered top-to-bottom-stacked windows.

Snap Layouts

Your active apps can be automatically arranged using the **Snap Layouts** feature. The options offered depend on the display resolution of your screen.

To adjust the **Snap Layout**:

 Hover the mouse pointer over the **Maximize** icon at the right of the **Title bar**

With a maximum screen resolution of 1920 x 1080 or higher, and with **Landscape** orientation, you will be offered these six arrangements:

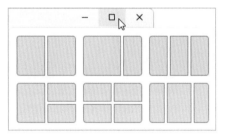

With a lower maximum screen resolution, you'll be given four arrangements to choose from:

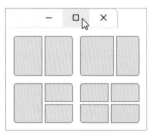

 Click your desired positioning, and the currently selected app will be moved to that location

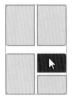

 You will then be able to select which of your active apps to place in each of the other locations in your chosen arrangement

Display resolution

To check the active resolution of your PC monitor:

 Right-click the **Start** button and select **Settings**, then select the **Display** entry on the **System** panel

 Scroll down to **Scale & Layout** where the display resolution is specified

You can also right-click a clear portion of the desktop and select **Display settings** from the list presented.

☐☐ View	>
↑↓ Sort by	>
↻ Refresh	
↩ Undo Rename	Ctrl+Z
⊕ New	>
⊡ Display settings	
⫽ Personalize	
▣ Open in Windows Terminal	
⬚ Show more options	Shift+F10

 Click the **Down** arrow to show the range of display resolutions that you could apply

1920 × 1080 (Recommended)
1680 × 1050
1600 × 900
1366 × 768
1280 × 1024
1280 × 720
1152 × 864
1024 × 768
800 × 600

The best setting is marked **Recommended**, and is the native and highest setting for your monitor. This is the setting that you should use in most situations.

If you select a lower resolution you'll be asked to specify whether you want to keep these display settings.

 Click **Keep changes** to apply the new setting, or select **Revert** to cancel the change

If you make no response, a countdown proceeds and, after 15 seconds, the display resolution automatically returns to its previous value.

Apps not being displayed run in the background (if supported) or get suspended. This lets them restart quickly. However, you may prefer to explicitly close unwanted apps.

Don't forget

If you are having problems closing a specific app, you can always run **Task Manager** by right-clicking on the **Start** button and selecting the **Task Manager** option. Once **Task Manager** is open, right-click on the app that is causing problems and select the **End task** option.

Closing apps

When apps are running in windowed mode, they feature the **Title bar** with its **Close** button.

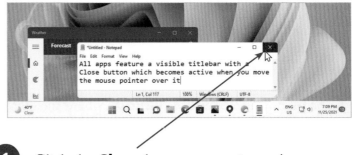

1 Click the **Close** button to terminate the app

When the app is running full-screen, it continues to display its Title bar, so you are still able to end the app by clicking its **Close** button.

You can also close an app by switching to that app and then pressing **Alt + F4**. Alternatively, with the app selected, press **Alt + Spacebar**. This displays the **Title bar** menu. Click on **Close** to close the app.

From the Taskbar, right-click the app icon and select **Close all windows**. This will immediately close all active instances of that app.

Alternatively, move the mouse pointer over the app icon until an app thumbnail appears, then click its **Close** button.

This method allows you to close a single instance of an app, when there are multiple copies active.

3 Windows 11 desktop

This chapter shows how Windows 11 still supports the traditional windowed desktop environment, including the Taskbar, Notifications area, and the familiar windows structure, menus and dialogs for managing desktop applications.

Desktop mode

Switch on your computer to start up Windows 11 and display the Lock screen (see page 24), and then sign in to your user account. The system will start up in **Desktop mode**.

The appearance of your desktop will vary depending on configuration and personalization, but you typically find:

Desktop icons   Active task   Background image

Taskbar shortcuts   Active task   Notifications area

Don't forget

Right-click **Start** then select **Settings** > **Personalization** > **Text input** and **Touch keyboard** to set the size of the Touch keyboard.

The **Touch keyboard** button appears on the Taskbar next to the **Notifications area**, for tablet PCs or for PCs with touch-enabled monitors attached.

Touch keyboard   Touch keyboard button

New desktop

In Windows 11, all apps run on the desktop – Universal as well as Classic Windows apps. To see how these appear:

1 Open a number of apps from the Start menu (see page 28) including, for example, an Office app

These app windows have been manually arranged, since the **Cascade windows** option has been removed from Windows 11.

If you have numerous apps open at once, you can organize them onto separate desktops.

2 Select the **Task View** button and click **New desktop** to create another desktop

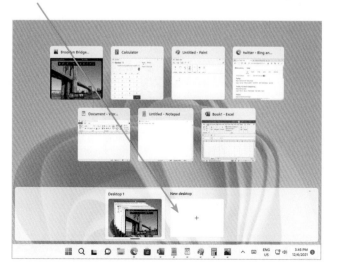

Press **WinKey + Ctrl + D** to create a new desktop and then switch to it immediately.

...cont'd

Press **WinKey** + **Tab** to open Task View with the contents of the active desktop displayed.

③ Click and drag an app in Task View and drop it onto the new desktop that has been created

④ Alternatively, right-click each desired app, click **Move to** and choose the target desktop

Snap left	
Snap right	
Move to >	Desktop 2
	New desktop

Task View shows the desktops that are defined, and the Taskbar shows the apps located on the selected desktop.

Hover the mouse pointer over a desktop to see its contents on the screen and on the Taskbar. Click on a specific desktop to make it the active desktop.

Taskbar

The contents of the Taskbar change dynamically to reflect the activities that are taking place on your desktop.

Taskbar shortcuts

At the left of the Taskbar is the **Start** button

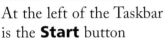

(the Windows logo button). To the right of this are the **Search**, the **Task View** and the app buttons – **Chat**, **File Explorer**, **Microsoft Edge**, and the **Microsoft Store**. These are apps provided by Microsoft. You can also pin your own choice of apps here.

The app icons turn into task buttons when you run the apps.

Task buttons

There is a task button for each active task. The selected task, in this case Excel, will be shown with a full underscore. An active

but not selected task such as **Calculator** has a shorter underscore. There is no underscore shown for apps that are not active, as with **Microsoft Store** in this example.

Notifications area

On the right of the Taskbar is the **Notifications area**, with the **Touch keyboard**,

Language, **Network** and **Speaker** buttons and the date and time value, plus the **Notifications counter** (if there are notifications waiting to be viewed).

If more than one input language is defined on your system, the **Language** button will list the languages installed and allow you to switch between them.

49

Taskbar properties

To make changes to the Taskbar properties:

1 Right-click an empty part of the Taskbar and click **Taskbar settings**, to open **Settings** at the Personalization > **Taskbar** panel

Don't forget

The Taskbar is located at the bottom edge, and may be positioned left or center, as detailed on page 31.

2 Scroll the list to display the **Taskbar behaviors** section, which offers more settings for the Taskbar

3 Click the **Automatically hide the taskbar** box

to make the full area of the screen available to app windows

Auto-hide the Taskbar to give more screen space.

4 The Taskbar reappears when you move the mouse pointer to the part of the screen where the Taskbar would otherwise have been located

5 Clear the **Automatically hide the taskbar** box, if you want the Taskbar to be displayed always

When your PC has multiple displays, you are offered the opportunity to show your Taskbar on all the displays.

Don't forget

Showing Taskbar apps on all Taskbars works best on higher-resolution screens, or with smaller numbers of active tasks.

51

With multiple displays, you also have the choice of showing your Taskbar apps on the Taskbars for all displays, or for specific displays only.

The main Taskbar shows the clock and tray icons and is on the main display. The clock and tray icons won't show on the Taskbars on the other displays.

Notifications

To make sure that you are aware of notifications as they become available:

1 Click the **Settings** button on the Taskbar

2 On the **System** panel that is displayed, scroll down to select **Notifications**

You can choose to turn Notifications **On** or **Off** for specific apps and other senders.

3 Ensure that the **Get notifications from apps and other senders** option is turned **On**

You can choose from **Show notifications on the lock screen**, **Show reminders and incoming VoIP calls on the lock screen** and **Allow notifications to play sounds** options

Scroll on down to request suggestions and tips on setting up your device and on using Windows, or select **Get help** to contact Microsoft Support.

Show desktop

When you have several applications running, their windows will obscure the actual desktop.

Don't forget

The **Win + D** key combination also performs **Show desktop** operations. Press once to reveal the desktop. Press again to restore the windows.

 Hover the mouse pointer over the far right of the Taskbar to reveal the **Show desktop** button, a narrow vertical line

If the **Show desktop** button isn't displayed, you can enable it in **Settings** > **Personalization** > **Taskbar** > **Taskbar behaviors**

2 Click the **Show desktop** button to hide the windows and show only the desktop and its icons

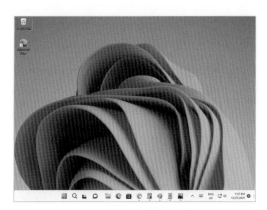

Hot tip

Click the **Show desktop** button a second time to redisplay the application windows.

The **Widgets** app is a new feature in Windows 11.

Click on this menu button for a specific widget, to access its menu for setting its size, and customizing it.

Small

Medium

• Large

✐ Customize widget

✕ Unpin widget

Widgets

The **Widgets** panel in Windows 11 contains a number of real-time items, such as newsfeeds and weather forecasts, that change as new information becomes available. The items in the **Widgets** panel are fully customizable. To use the **Widgets** panel:

1 Click on this button on the Taskbar
71°F
Mostly cloudy

2 The **Widgets** panel is displayed, with the default widgets. Click on a widget to display more comprehensive information about the item (opens in the **Edge** browser)

3 Scroll down the page to view the rest of the available widgets, and their content

David Bowie to Be Honored With a Stone Disc on London's Music Walk of Fame

What To Plant In Your Fall Garden — & What To Cook With Your Crop

4 Move the cursor over a widget and click on this button in the top right-hand corner to close (hide) a widget

5 Click on the account button in the top right-hand corner of the **Widgets** panel, to access the **Widgets settings** panel. Click on categories to add them, or click on the **Manage interests** option

6 Options for managing the items that appear in the **Widgets** panel are displayed. The left-hand panel contains the categories of subjects that can be included. The main window contains a Search box, and the most frequently used categories

Click on the **+** button next to a category in Step 6 to follow that category so that it is included in the **Widgets** panel.

7 Click on an item in the left-hand panel to view its options in the main window, and add them to the **Widgets** panel, as required

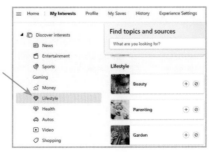

Don't forget

55

Desktop icons

Shortcuts to any Windows application can be stored on the desktop. To start with, there are standard system icons.

You can change desktop icons from the default size (**Medium**) to **Large** as shown here, or to **Small**. You can also change their size by pressing the **Ctrl** key and scrolling the mouse wheel, to vary between very small and very large.

 To display or resize icons on the desktop, right-click an empty part of the desktop and select **View**

Click the **Change Icon...** button in Step 4 to select alternative images for any of the system icons. Click **Restore Default** to revert to the original images.

2 If the **Show desktop icons** entry is not already selected (checked), then click to enable it

3 Select **Personalize** from the right-click menu, and choose **Themes > Desktop icon settings**

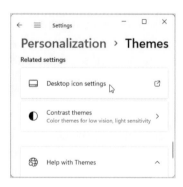

4 Select icons that you wish to display, then click **OK** to apply the changes

For quick access, you can add shortcuts to the Taskbar for both Classic and Universal apps.

1 Select the **Search** icon on the Taskbar and type an app name; e.g. "notepad.exe"

2 Right-click the result to display the context menu and select **Pin to taskbar**

3 View the Taskbar to see a shortcut for the app

Don't forget

You can also right-click the entry for the app in the **All apps** list and select **More** to find **Pin to taskbar**.

You can now run the app from the Taskbar. However, if you prefer, you can create an app shortcut on the desktop, where there's room for lots of application shortcuts.

1 Search for an app in the Search box on the Start menu. Right-click on the required app, and select **Open file location**

2 **File Explorer** opens with the app file selected

3 Right-click on the app and click on the **Copy** icon

4 Access the desktop and right-click. Click on the **Paste** icon

5 You can now run the app from the desktop by double-clicking that shortcut icon

...cont'd

You can also create shortcuts on the desktop using drag and drop from the **All apps** list, for both Classic and Universal apps.

1. Scroll to an app in the **All apps** list, such as the **Calculator** app

2. Select and drag the app icon onto the desktop, and release it when a **Link** flag appears

3. Similarly, scroll to another app such as **Weather**, and drag and drop it onto the desktop

You can add other **Windows Accessories** such as **Notepad** and **Paint** (see pages 119 and 122), applications such as **Word** and **Excel** from the **Microsoft Office** suite, and Universal apps such as **Money**.

You can drag the desktop shortcut icons to arrange them in groups according to type, perhaps, or by project or activity. If you have many icons on your desktop, you can group them in folders (see page 76) to make them easier to locate.

Window structure

When you open a folder, or start a Windows function or application program on the desktop, it appears as a window that can be moved and resized. For example:

1 Click the **WordPad** icon found in **Windows Tools** in the **All apps** list

Not all the Windows applications use the Ribbon style. See page 60 for Notepad, an example of a simpler window.

Features of a typical application window

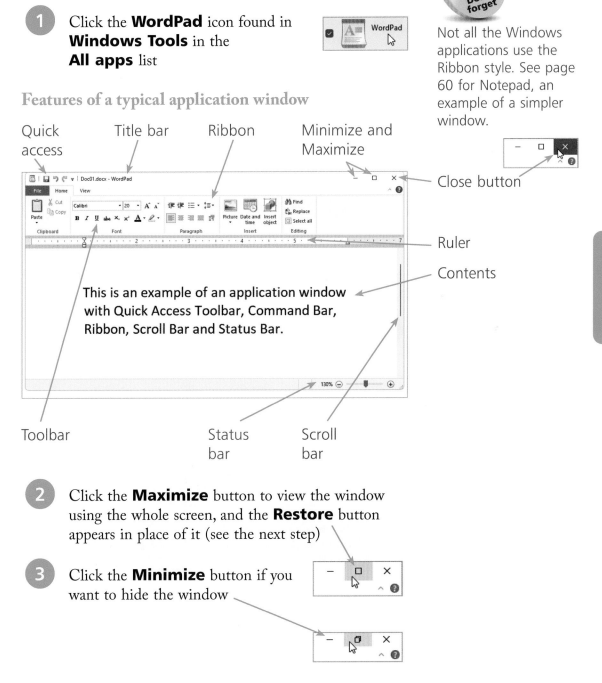

Quick access

Title bar

Ribbon

Minimize and Maximize

Close button

Ruler

Contents

This is an example of an application window with Quick Access Toolbar, Command Bar, Ribbon, Scroll Bar and Status Bar.

Toolbar

Status bar

Scroll bar

2 Click the **Maximize** button to view the window using the whole screen, and the **Restore** button appears in place of it (see the next step)

3 Click the **Minimize** button if you want to hide the window

Application windows

Even in Windows 11, application programs may still use the traditional window structure, with a **Title bar** and **Menu bar**. For example, see the **Notepad** application:

1 Select **Start** > **All apps** > **Notepad**

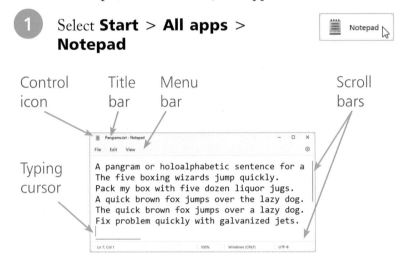

Control icon   Title bar   Menu bar   Scroll bars

Typing cursor

Other Windows 11 applications such as **WordPad** and **Paint** use the Scenic Ribbon in place of the **Menu bar**.

1 Select **Start** > **All apps** > **Windows Tools** and **WordPad**

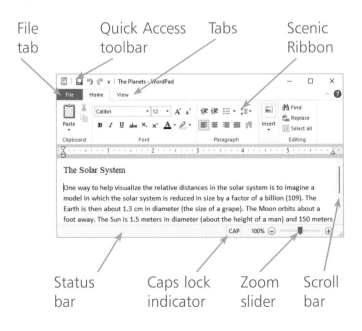

File tab   Quick Access toolbar   Tabs   Scenic Ribbon

Status bar   Caps lock indicator   Zoom slider   Scroll bar

Menus and dialogs

The entries on **Command bars**, **Menu bars** and **Ribbons** expand to provide a list of related options to choose from. Some entries expand into a sub-menu; for example:

 Open Notepad from **All apps** and click **View** on the **Menu bar** to display the options, then hover over **Zoom** to display its sub-set of options

 Open **WordPad** from Windows Tools and **All apps** and click **Editing** on the Ribbon to see its options

61

Some commands open dialog boxes that allow you to apply detailed configurations and settings. For example:

 Open **WordPad** as above and select **File**, then choose **Page Setup**

You are presented with a panel where you can adjust the way that pages are handled during printing.

 Click **OK** to confirm and apply any changes that you have made

Moving and resizing windows

 To maximize a window, double-click the **Title bar** area (double-click again to restore the window to its original size)

 To move a window, click the **Title bar** area, hold down the mouse button and drag the window

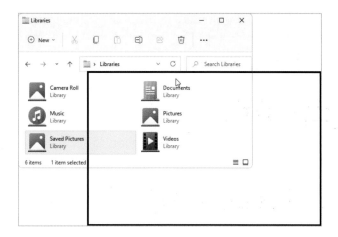

 To resize a window, move the mouse pointer over any border or any corner

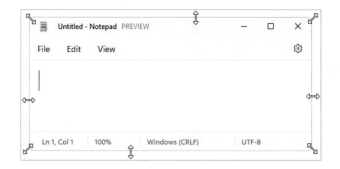

 When the desired double-headed **Resize** arrow appears, click and drag until the frame displayed is the required size

5 Release the pointer and the window is resized

4 Personalizing your system

In this chapter you will learn how to change the appearance of the Windows 11 Lock screen and Start menu, add an account picture, organize the apps, manage your user account, and add a picture, a password or a PIN code. You can also personalize the desktop environment and manage the display options, including screen resolution and also using the Accessibility options for ease of access.

Some of the settings have been updated in Windows 11.

Settings

Windows 11 provides the **Settings** function to make changes to your system. There are several ways to open **Settings**:

 Click on the **Settings** app on the Taskbar

 Press **WinKey** + **I** to open **Settings** directly

 Press **WinKey** + **X**, or right-click on the **Start** button and select **Settings**

 Click on the **Start** button and click on **All apps**. Select **Settings** from the alphabetic list

5 However the settings are accessed, the main categories appear in the left-hand sidebar. Click on a main category to view its content in the main **Settings** window

Settings categories

The categories of settings, accessed from the left-hand panel of the Settings app are:

- **System**. These settings provide numerous options to specify how your computer looks and operates.

- **Bluetooth & devices**. These settings provide settings for how the hardware connected with your computer operates.

- **Network & internet**. These settings provide settings related to connecting to networks, usually for accessing the internet.

- **Personalization**. These settings provide options for customizing the look and feel of Windows 11.

- **Apps**. These settings provide options for specifying how apps work and interact with Windows 11.

- **Accounts**. These settings provide options for adding new online accounts (such as a new email account, or an online storage and sharing service).

- **Time & language**. These settings provide options for the time zone used by your computer, and the format for these items.

- **Gaming**. These settings contain a range of options for playing games on a Windows 11 computer.

- **Accessibility**. These settings are divided into three sections, for **Vision**, **Hearing** and **Interaction**.

- **Privacy & security**. These settings can be used for a wide range of options for managing your data, and also security settings for keeping your computer as well protected as possible.

- **Windows Update**. These settings provide options for installing updates to Windows, and also backing up and recovering data on your computer.

...cont'd

Working with settings

It is worth spending some time with the settings, as they can be invaluable in terms of managing Windows 11 and also customizing it so that you can create a look and feel with which you are most comfortable. To find your way around the settings:

 Click on a category in the left-hand sidebar of the **Settings** app to view its details in the main window

 Click on a right-pointing arrow to access more options for a specific setting

 Drag buttons **On** or **Off** to apply or disable specific settings

 Click on the left-pointing arrow in the top left-hand corner of the **Settings** window to go back to the previous page being viewed in the **Settings** app

Hot tip

If the left-hand navigation panel in the **Settings** app is not visible (for instance, if the window has been reduced in size by resizing) click on this button on the top toolbar to view the navigation sidebar.

Quick Settings

The **Quick Settings** feature is an easy way to change some of the settings on your PC. To display **Quick Settings**:

 Click the Taskbar near the Wi-Fi icon and the Volume icon (or press the **WinKey** + **A** key combination)

The contents of **Quick Settings** depend on the particular system. This example shows the entries for a typical desktop PC.

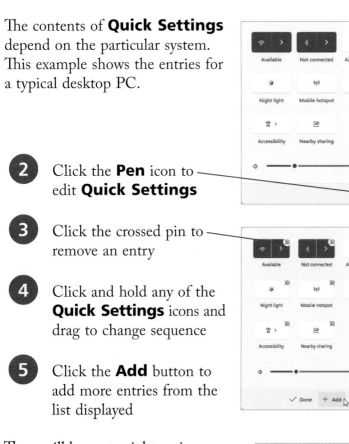

2 Click the **Pen** icon to edit **Quick Settings**

3 Click the crossed pin to remove an entry

4 Click and hold any of the **Quick Settings** icons and drag to change sequence

5 Click the **Add** button to add more entries from the list displayed

There will be up to eight options offered for display on the **Quick Settings** panel.

 Click the **Done** button when you have finished editing the settings

Don't forget

The options offered will vary, depending on the device features and the level of current updates.

The **Focus** function is a new feature in Windows 11. It replaces the **Focus Assist** and **Quiet Hours** features of previous Windows versions.

Even if **do not disturb** is turned on, apps can still be given permission to use notifications. This can be done in **Settings** > **System** > **Notifications** > **Set priority notifications**.

Keeping focus

How you receive notifications can be personalized to ensure that you only get them when you want, using the **Focus** function. To do this:

 Open the **Settings** app and click on the **Focus** option within the **System** section

 Details about the potential focus session are displayed. These include showing and hiding certain functions and turning on **do not disturb** so that you do not receive notifications from any of your apps (unless they have been given permission; see the Hot tip)

System > **Focus**

Focus sessions help you get more done by reducing distractions. When you start a session, these settings will apply for a set amount of time.

ⓞ Focus	▶ Start focus session ⌃
Session duration	— 30 mins +

☑ Show the timer in the Clock app

☑ Hide badges on taskbar apps

☑ Hide flashing on taskbar apps

☑ Turn on do not disturb

⑦ More about focus

3 Click on the **-** and **+** buttons to set the duration for the focus session and click on the **Start focus session** button

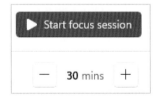

4 Click on the **Stop focus session** button to stop the focus settings being applied

Personalizing the Lock screen

The **Lock** screen appears when you start Windows 11, sign out, or resume from sleep. To customize this screen:

1 Open **Settings** then select the **Personalization > Lock screen** option

You can also open the **Personalization** settings by right-clicking the desktop and selecting the **Personalize** option.

2 Scroll down and select one of the supplied pictures as the image for your **Lock** screen

You can choose to display all the contents of your **Pictures** library in the form of a slideshow that runs on the **Lock** screen. This is accessed from the **Personalize your lock screen** option at the top of the window.

3 Alternatively, click **Browse photos** to select an image from your **Pictures** library or another image folder

4 Select the required picture and click **Choose picture**

The picture you select can also appear on the **Sign in** screen.

...cont'd

You can view your changes to the **Lock** screen immediately. To do this:

 Select the **Start** button and right-click the user icon on the Start menu

 Select **Lock** to display the **Lock** screen, whilst still retaining your current session

You don't have to save the changes or close the **Settings** function to apply any changes. The updates will be applied immediately.

Click the **Tips** link to visit the **Windows Resource Center** where you'll be offered a variety of informative documents, including – for example – an introduction to the Windows 11 operating system.

Desktop

1 Select **Settings** >
Personalization >
Background

2 Choose **Picture** from the drop-down menu and select an image to act as the background for the desktop

3 You can click **Browse photos**, and select an image from your Pictures library or another image folder

4 Select **Personalization** > **Start** to control which items are shown on the Start menu

5 Select **Personalization** > **Colors** to apply a color accent to the Taskbar, window borders and Start menu

6 Select **Fonts** to display the fonts available on your system and get more fonts from the Microsoft Store

7 Select **Themes** to apply predefined sets of colors, images and sound effects, and other related settings

Beware

If you are signed in with a Microsoft account, your choices will be applied to any Windows 11 PC you sign in to with that Microsoft account.

Don't forget

Background can be set as a picture, a slideshow or simply a solid color. The image may be made to fill the screen; fit to height; stretch both ways; tile; center; or span across multiple monitors.

71

Don't forget

Each username will have the default user image assigned, but this can be replaced by a more suitable image.

Don't forget

You can specify a picture of any size, but preferably a square image, and it will be reconstructed for use when signing in, etc.

Account picture

You can specify an image that will be displayed with your username wherever it appears.

 Right-click your username on the Start menu, and click **Change account settings**

 Alternatively, open **Settings** > **Accounts** > **Your info**

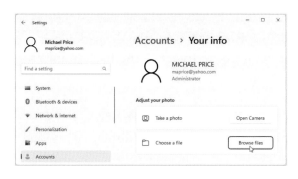

 Click **Browse files** to select an existing image from your **Pictures** library or another image folder

 Alternatively, if your computer has a webcam or built-in camera, select **Camera** to take a picture

5 You can create a still photo or you can take a short video, which is limited to five seconds in length

6 Press the **WinKey** to see the effect on the Start menu. Press the **WinKey** again to return to **Settings**

Managing the Start menu

The apps initially pinned to your Start menu depend on choices made by the manufacturer or supplier of your computer, and will be in no particular sequence. However, you can add and remove apps to suit your requirements.

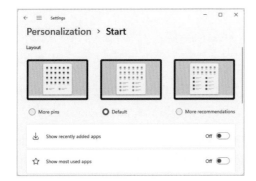

Turn on the **Show recently added apps** option, which will appear in the **Recommended** section.

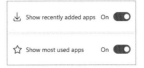

You can also choose **Show most used apps**, at the top of the **All apps** list.

To customize the Start menu:

1 Select **Settings > Personalization > Start**

2 You can accept the **Default** option, choose **More pins** to see more apps, or select **More recommendations** (and therefore fewer pinned apps)

...cont'd

Don't forget

You can add your own folders to the Start menu. Right-click the folder in **File Explorer** (see Chapter 5) and select **Pin to Start**.

3 Select the **Folders** option within **Start**

> 📁 Folders
> These folders appear on Start next to the Power button
> ⟩

4 Choose which of the system folders you'd like to appear on the Start menu

← ≡ Settings   — ☐ ✕

Personalization › Start › **Folders**

Choose which folders appear on Start next to the Power button.

⚙️ Settings	On ⬤
📁 File Explorer	Off ◯
📄 Documents	On ⬤
↓ Downloads	Off ◯
♪ Music	On ⬤
🖼 Pictures	On ⬤
▣ Videos	Off ◯
🌐 Network	On ⬤
📇 Personal folder	Off ◯

🔍 Get help
💬 Give feedback

Hot tip

You can right-click the row of icons on the Start menu and select **Personalize this list**, to redisplay the folders and revise your choice.

5 Click the **On/Off** button to display/hide the icon for each of the folders

The icons for the chosen folders are displayed at the foot of the Start menu, next to the **Power** button.

R Michael Price   📄 ♪ ▣ 🌐 ⚙️ ⏻

Managing apps

Right-click apps pinned to the Start menu to see which actions are offered.

 1 Select the **Paint** app and you'll be offered a set of six actions including **Unpin from Start**, **Pin to taskbar** and **Uninstall**

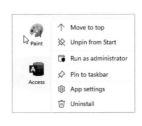

2 If the app is not already on the Start menu, you'll be offered **Pin to Start** rather than **Unpin from Start**

⚲ Pin to Start

3 Select **Microsoft Access** (if installed) and you'll again see six actions, but with **Open file location** in place of **App settings**

4 For applications such as **Maps** or **Photos**, you will see just four actions

 5 If you have a folder entry pinned to the Start menu, you can right-click and select **Move to top**, **Unpin from Start** or **Open file location**

6 Right-click an entry in the **Recommended** section of the Start menu to get the **Remove from list** option

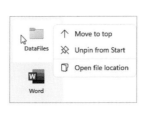

▢ Open file location

✕ Remove from list

Don't forget

You can add items from the desktop to the Start menu, such as disks, libraries and folders. Right-click the item in **File Explorer** and select **Pin to Start** from the menu.

When you add new apps from the Store, or install applications such as Microsoft Office, they are added to the **All apps** list, in their alphabetical sequence.

Grouping apps

Support for named groups and folders of apps has been removed from Windows 11. However, there is a way to achieve a similar effect.

 Add a shortcut to the desktop for the **Access** application, using drag and drop from the **All apps** list (see page 58)

 Repeat this procedure to create shortcuts for the other **Office** applications

 Right-click the desktop and select **New** > **Folder**. Name that folder "MS-Office"

 Drag and drop each of the Office application shortcuts in turn into the new folder

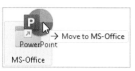

You'll now have a folder on the desktop that contains shortcuts for all of the applications in Microsoft Office.

Double-click the folder icon to open it and reveal its contents.

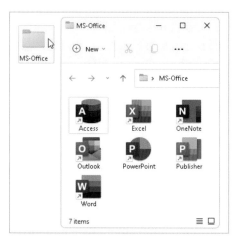

You can pin the folder to the Start menu, to give easy access to the group of Microsoft Office applications.

1 Right-click the folder icon on the desktop and select **Pin to Start**

The link to the folder will be added to the Start menu, as the last entry in **Pinned**.

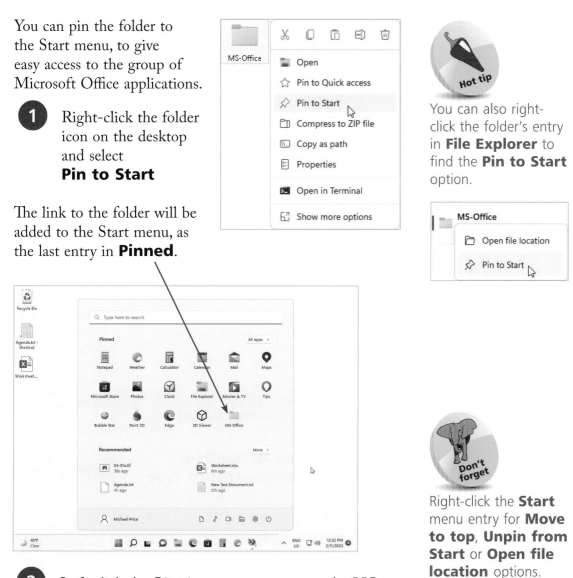

2 Left-click the **Start** menu entry to open the **MS-Office** folder

3 Click any entry on the Start menu, and drag it anywhere you wish

Using the click and drag method, you can organize entries on the Start menu in any order you wish, to make things easier to locate.

Hot tip

You can also right-click the folder's entry in **File Explorer** to find the **Pin to Start** option.

Don't forget

Right-click the **Start** menu entry for **Move to top**, **Unpin from Start** or **Open file location** options.

User accounts

To allow several users to share the same PC, you give everyone their own sign-in (username and password) and access to their own files, browsers and desktop settings.

Each user could have a Local account, just for that one PC, or a Microsoft account that can be used on any PC on your network. The accounts you create will be of two types: **Standard** or **Administrator**.

Standard account

By default, when you create an account it will be a **Standard** account that can use most apps and change basic system settings that do not affect other users.

Administrator account

This is an elevated account that has complete access to the PC and can make account type changes and modifications to the system that can impact all users.

To list user accounts:

 Click Start, type "control panel" and select the **Control Panel** app

See page 92 for information about opening the **Control Panel**.

 Select **User Accounts** and click **Change account type**

All of the user accounts defined on the PC are displayed, with the username, account type, administrator status (if applicable), and whether the account is password-protected.

 Click the **Close** button at the top right to exit **Manage Accounts**

Hot tip

Changing the user account

 1 Select **Settings** > **Accounts** > **Your info**

2 If you are signed in with a Local account, you can switch to a Microsoft account instead

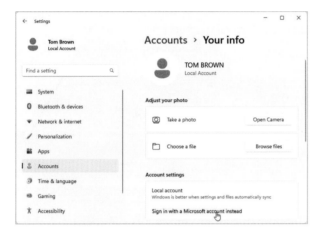

3 If you are signed in with a Microsoft account, you can switch to a Local account instead

4 In either case, you can change your password, create a picture password, create a PIN or add a new user account (see pages 80-81)

You'll be asked to provide an email address, which may be for an existing Microsoft account, or one that can be used to create such an account.

You must provide a username, password and password hint to aid signing in to this computer. Note that as a Local account, it will not be synced with your other Windows computers.

PIN is an acronym for Personal Identification Number, and is usually a four-digit code (see page 86 for options).

New user account

1 Select **Settings** > **Accounts** > **Family** > **Add someone**

Hot tip

You can add other users as part of your Family group, giving them an account of their own with libraries and standard folders.

Don't forget

If the new user does not already have a Microsoft account, you can create one as part of the process of adding the user's account.

2 Provide the email address for the person's Microsoft account and click **Next**

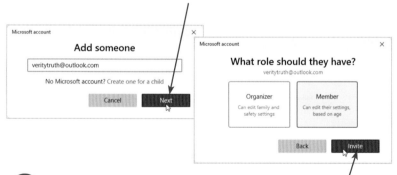

Don't forget

The username is added to the list of users shown on the **Sign in** screen.

3 Select a role for the new person, and click **Invite** to offer the option to join your Family group

4 The new user receives an email with the invitation to join the Family group

5 The user should click **Accept Invitation** to join the group. No action need be taken if the decision is not to join

...cont'd

You can add non-family members to the **Other Users** section of **Accounts**.

 1 Select **Settings** > **Accounts** > **Other Users** > **Add account**

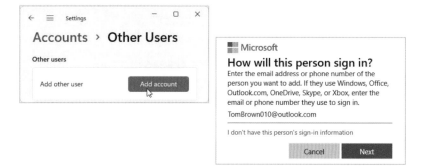

You may find on your system that you must select **Family & Other Users** to locate the **Other Users** option.

 2 Follow the prompts, providing the user's email details when requested, to add the new user

This user will be able to sign in to the PC, even if the existing account remains logged on to the computer.

 3 From the Start menu, the new user should click the current user and select their name from the list

4 On the **Sign in** screen that appears, type the password and press the **Enter** button

Windows creates user libraries and folders and installs any necessary apps. Progress messages are displayed. When setup completes, Windows returns with the new user account active and ready for use.

If you sign out, switch users or shut down and restart, the new user account can be selected from the **Sign in** screen.

81

Setting up a Kiosk

With a PC set up as a **Kiosk**, you restrict the computer to a single Universal app. This is perhaps an alternative to the **Guest** user, which was offered in systems prior to Windows 10.

1 Select **Settings** > **Accounts** > **Family & other users** (or **Other Users**) to find **Set up a kiosk**

Set up a kiosk

Kiosk
Turn this device into a kiosk to use as a digital sign, interactive display, or other things

Get started

2 Click **Get started** and enter a name for your Kiosk account, then click the **Next** button

Create an account

We'll help you create an account that will automatically sign in on start up.

Add a name

MyKiosk

Choose an existing account

Next   Cancel

Choose a kiosk app

This is the only app that can be used in kiosk mode.

Help me pick the right app

Solitaire Collection
Microsoft Studios

SupportAssist
Dell Inc

Tips
Microsoft Corporation

Voice Recorder
Microsoft Corporation

Weather
Microsoft Corporation

Next   Cancel

3 Choose an app that is to be used on the Kiosk, then click **Next**. In this case, **Solitaire Collection** is selected

Access to the specified app is now defined for the Kiosk computer.

You're done!

To use this device as a kiosk, sign in with the account you just set up.

When you're in kiosk mode, use Ctrl+Alt+Delete to exit.

Close   Cancel

Don't forget

It isn't essential to restart your PC to apply the changes and make the newly defined account available for use.

4 Click the **Close** button to finish

5 To try out the Kiosk computer, sign out or restart the system so that it displays the **Lock** screen

6 Select or swipe up on the **Lock** screen to display the **Sign in** screen

7 Select the **MyKiosk** account – no password will be required

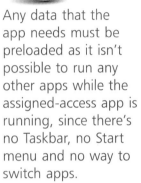

8 The system starts up with the defined app displayed, ready for use

Any data that the app needs must be preloaded as it isn't possible to run any other apps while the assigned-access app is running, since there's no Taskbar, no Start menu and no way to switch apps.

In this example, the Kiosk computer can run any of the nine Solitaire games included in the collection, but no other programs are available to be run.

To terminate your use of the Kiosk account, enter the **Ctrl + Alt + Del** key combination to return to the **Sign in** screen, where you can switch users.

To finish completely, left click the **Power** symbol and select **Shut down**. Other options include **Sleep** and **Restart**. If there are updates pending, you may be offered **Update and shut down** or **Update and restart** options.

Picture password

Don't forget

You'd normally use picture passwords with a touchscreen, but it is possible to use a mouse.

1 Select **Settings** > **Accounts** > **Sign-in options**

2 Click **Add** for **Picture password**

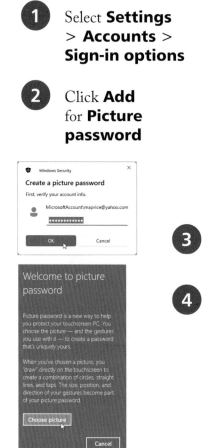

Don't forget

A picture password consists of three gestures, applied in sequence at specific locations. You can choose one or more types of gesture – draw a circle, draw a straight line or tap the screen at a point.

3 Type your password to verify the account, then click **OK**

4 Select **Choose picture**, locate the file you require, then click **Open**

5 Follow the prompts to position the picture, draw the three gestures and confirm your gestures

Hot tip

If needed, you can start over to enter a new set of gestures, if you are having trouble repeating your initial selection.

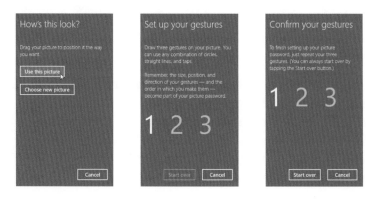

6 When you've successfully confirmed your gestures and your picture password is set up, click **Finish**

The selected gestures – a tap, a line and a circle – are shown here for illustration purposes, but such indicators do not normally appear on the display, except when you are having problems during the initial setup.

The next time the **Lock** screen appears and you sign in, you'll be able to use your picture password.

You can use **Windows Hello** to sign in if your PC is set up for it. Go to Start, then select **Settings** > **Accounts** > **Sign-in options**. Under **Windows Hello**, you'll see **Facial recognition**, **Fingerprint recognition**, and **Iris recognition** options if your PC has a fingerprint reader or a camera that supports it. Once you're set up, you'll be able to use **Windows Hello** to sign in.

7 Select **Sign-in options** to switch to the PIN or the password sign-in procedure

Don't forget

PIN codes are usually four digits and meant for tablet PCs, but can be used with any Windows 11 PC. You can use letters and symbols as well as digits (up to 127 characters in total).

Hot tip

You can return to **Sign-in options** at any time to change your PIN code, to remove the PIN as a sign-in option, or to reset a forgotten PIN code.

PIN code

1 Select **Settings > Accounts > Sign-in options** and **PIN (Windows Hello)**, and then select **Set up**

2 Click **Next** to create a PIN (and enter your Microsoft password if prompted)

3 Enter four or more digits for the PIN and re-enter the numbers to confirm the PIN code

4 Select **OK** when the values have been entered

When you next sign in, you'll be asked for the PIN, which you can enter by keyboard or touch. You just provide the code itself – there's no need to press the **Enter** key.

The PIN codes and picture passwords that you define will apply only to the particular computer on which they have been specified, and will not be transferred to any other computer on which you may choose to enable your Microsoft account.

Display settings

1 Right-click the desktop and select **Display settings** from the list

> 🖵 Display settings
> ✏ Personalize

System › Display

Brightness & color

Brightness
Adjust the brightness of the built-in display

Night light
Use warmer colors to help block blue light   Off

HDR
More about HDR

Hot tip

You can open **Settings**, select **System**, and then choose **Display**, or you can type "display" in the Search box and select **Display settings** from the results shown.

> 🔍 display settings
>
> **Best match**
>
> 🖵 **Display settings**
>   System settings

2 Adjust the brightness of the display, turn on **Night light**, and enable **HDR** (high dynamic range) – if supported by your computer

3 Scroll down for more options

System › Display

Scale & layout

Scale
Change the size of text, apps, and other items

100% (Recommended)

Display resolution
Adjust the resolution to fit your connected display

1920 × 1080 (Recommended)

Display orientation   Landscape

Multiple displays
Choose the presentation mode for your displays

Don't forget

Screens emit blue light, which may be less comfortable at night, so you can turn on **Night light** in Step 1 and your monitor will display warmer colors.

4 A scaling factor for text and apps will be recommended, but you can change this to suit your preference

| 100% (Recommended) |
| 125% |
| 150% |
| 175% |

...cont'd

Beware

The resolutions, color settings and connections offered depend on the type of monitor and the type of graphics adapter that you have on your computer.

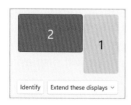

Don't forget

The screen thumbnails will change to reflect resolution and orientation changes. You can also drag and drop the thumbnails to match the physical organization.

5 Click the **Display resolution** box to see the alternatives available

| 1080 × 1920 |
| 1050 × 1680 (Recommended) |
| 1024 × 1280 |
| 864 × 1152 |
| 800 × 1280 |
| 768 × 1024 |
| 720 × 1280 |
| 600 × 800 |

6 Choose a new resolution that you want to use, if the recommendation option doesn't suit your requirements

The higher the resolution, the more information you will fit on the screen, but of course the text and images displayed will be smaller.

7 Click the **Display orientation** box to select **Landscape** or **Portrait**. Either can be flipped if appropriate

| Landscape |
| Portrait |
| Landscape (flipped) |
| Portrait (flipped) |

Adjustments to **Brightness**, **Night light** or **Scaling** will be applied immediately, but when revisions of any other settings are applied, you will be asked to confirm that you want to keep the changes you have made.

1 If you want to retain the display settings as shown, click **Keep changes**

Keep these display settings?

Reverting to previous display settings in 11 seconds.

| Keep changes | Revert |

2 To undo the changes, select **Revert**, or simply wait 15 seconds and the changes will be reversed

Accessibility settings

Making Windows 11 accessible for as wide a range of users as possible is an important consideration, and there are a range of accessibility settings that can be used for this. To configure these:

 1 Open **Settings** and click on the **Accessibility** tab

 2 Select options in the main panel. The main headings are for **Vision**, **Hearing** and **Interaction**

Accessibility
Vision
AA Text size — Text size that appears throughout Windows and your apps >
Visual effects — Scroll bars, transparency, animations, notification timeout >
Mouse pointer and touch — Mouse pointer color, size >
Text cursor — Appearance and thickness, text cursor indicator >
Magnifier — Magnifier reading, zoom increment >
Color filters — Colorblindness filters, grayscale, inverted >
Contrast themes — Color themes for low vision, light sensitivity >
Narrator — Voice, verbosity, keyboard, braille >

3 Each option has settings that can be applied. For instance, drag the **Narrator** button from **Off** to **On** to enable items to be read out on the screen

Accessibility › Narrator
Narrator is a screen reader that describes what's on your screen.
Use Narrator
Narrator — On ⬤ ⌄
Keyboard shortcut for Narrator — Press the Windows logo key ⊞ + Ctrl + Enter to turn Narrator on and off — On ⬤
Narrator Home — Get help, access settings, and learn about new Narrator features — ⌄
Complete guide to Narrator — ⧉
Narrator's voice
Voice — Microsoft David - English (United States) ⌄
Add voices — >
Speed — Press Narrator + Plus (+) or Narrator + Minus (-) to change voice speed — − ⬤ +

The **Accessibility** settings have been renamed in Windows 11, from **Ease of Access**.

Don't forget

The settings for **Narrator** can be used to specify items on the screen that are read out. For some items, such as buttons and controls, there is an audio description of the item.

Don't forget

There is also a **Braille** option that can be accessed toward the bottom of the **Narrator** window. This has to be used in conjunction with third-party software that communicates with a Braille display.

...cont'd

4 Select **Magnifier** in Step 2 on page 89, and turn Magnifier **On** to activate the magnifying glass. Move this over areas of the screen to magnify them

Hot tip

To make the typing cursor easier to spot, select **Text cursor** in the **Vision** section and drag the **Size** slider to suit your needs.

You can also adjust the thickness value of the text cursor, and choose a color that stands out in your text.

5 Select the **Contrast themes** option in Step 2 on page 89, and click in the **Contrast themes** box to select a color theme for text and background for users who find it difficult reading black text on a white background

6 In the **Hearing** section, click on the **Captions** option then drag the **Live captions** button **On** to enable captions for compatible audio and video content

The **Vision** settings are: Text size, Visual effects, Mouse pointer and touch, Text cursor, Magnifier, Color filters, Contrast themes, and Narrator. The **Hearing** settings are: Audio and Captions. The **Interaction** settings are: Speech, Keyboard, Mouse, and Eye control.

 7 In the **Interaction** section, select **Mouse** to choose to use the numeric keypad to move the mouse, and adjust the color, size and speed of the mouse pointer

Opening the Control Panel

In previous versions of Windows, the most comprehensive options for customizing your system were provided via the **Control Panel**. Although the **Settings** feature is gradually taking over, the **Control Panel** is still used for some functions, although it is more hidden away these days. To access the **Control Panel**:

 Click on the **Search** icon on the Taskbar

 Enter "control panel" in the Search box. When the **Control Panel** entry appears, click it or press **Enter**

Best match

Control Panel
App

Hot tip

Another way to access the **Control Panel** is to select **Windows Tools** from the **All apps** list and click on the **Control Panel** option.

Options for the **Control Panel** are displayed

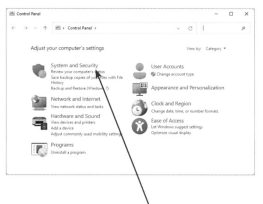

Don't forget

Click on the **Category** button in the top right of the **Control Panel** window to select options for how items in the **Control Panel** are displayed.

 Click on one of the main categories to view its contents

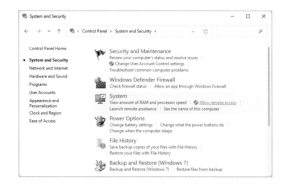

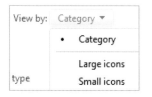

5 Searching and organizing

Windows 11 helps organize the files and folders on your hard disk. Content is stored in separate folders for different types of files, or you can add new folders. Libraries allow you to work with a group of folders. Powerful search facilities help you find your way around folders and menus.

File Explorer

Although **File Explorer** is not necessarily one of the first apps that you will use with Windows 11, it still plays an important role in organizing your folders and files. To access **File Explorer**:

 From the desktop, click on this icon on the Taskbar, or

Beware

This PC displays files from different locations as a single collection, without actually moving any files.

94

Hot tip

You can click on the **Start** button and access **File Explorer** from here too.

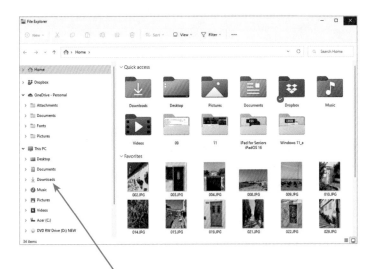 Press **WinKey + E**, and **File Explorer** opens at the **Home** folder

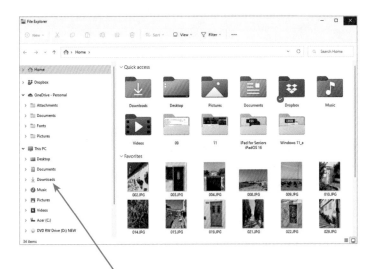 The locations on the computer are shown in the left-hand navigation pane

File Explorer Menu bar

The **Menu bar** in **File Explorer** has been simplified in Windows 11, replacing the **Scenic Ribbon**, but it can still be used for a variety of tasks for viewing and managing items within **File Explorer**.

 The **Menu bar** is displayed at the top of **File Explorer**, regardless of which window is being viewed. If nothing is selected in **File Explorer**, a number of options are unavailable (grayed out)

The **File Explorer Menu bar** has been updated in Windows 11.

 Click on an item within a **File Explorer** window to activate more of the options on the **Menu bar**

3 Click on the down-pointing arrow next to an item in the **Menu bar** to access its additional options for the current **File Explorer** window

Right-click anywhere within a **File Explorer** window to access the **File Explorer** context menu; i.e. one that applies to the item in the current window.

4 Click on this button (**See more**) to view more options for a selected item

Files and folders

The hardware components are the building blocks for your computer, but it is the information on your hard disk that really makes your computer operate. There is a huge number of files and folders stored there, in **File Explorer**. To get an idea of how many:

1 Right-click **This PC** on the desktop and select **Open**

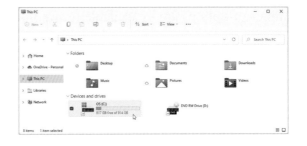

2 When **File Explorer** opens, double-click the **OS (C:)** drive to reveal its contents

3 Press **Ctrl** + **A** to select all items in the specified drive

4 Right-click the selection and click **Properties**

5 In this example, you see quoted counts of over 316,000 files and almost 70,000 folders on the **C:** drive, not including any hidden items

...cont'd

With so many files and folders to handle, they must be well organized to ensure that you can locate documents, pictures and other data you require with ease. Windows helps by grouping its files into related sections; for example:

- **Program Files**   Application programs (64-bit).
- **Program Files (x86)** Application programs (32-bit).
- **Program Data**   Application data files (hidden).
- **Users**   Documents, pictures, etc.
- **Windows**   Operating system files & data.

These are top-level folders on your hard disk and each one is divided into sub-folders. For example, the **Program Files** folders are arranged by supplier and application.

1   Open the **C:** drive, then double-click **Program Files**, **Adobe**, then **Acrobat DC**, and select **Acrobat**

2   Note that in the Navigation pane you see an arrow symbol in front of most of the folders

A gray arrow symbol (**›**) indicates there are sub-folders within that folder.

A black symbol (**∨**) implies that the folder is at least partially expanded.

Hot tip

The **Users** folder contains a folder for each user defined on the computer (see page 98). Each user folder contains **Documents**, **Pictures**, **Music** and other sub-folders.

Hot tip

There are **Forward** and **Back** arrows on the Address bar that allow you to retrace movements between folders.

The **Down** arrow lists recent locations. The **Up** arrow takes you to the desktop.

User folders

Documents and pictures that you create or save on your computer are kept in folders associated with your username.

1 Open the **C:** drive in **File Explorer** (see page 96), then select and double-click the **Users** folder

The **Public** folder is available to all user accounts and can be used to share files with other people using the same computer or using other computers on the same network. To share with any internet-connected computer or device, use **OneDrive** (see pages 100-103).

2 You'll see a sub-folder for each user account name, plus the **Public** sub-folder

3 Double-click the folder for the active user – in this example, John Smith

There is a set of sub-folders with all documents, pictures, data files and settings belonging to that user. There's also a link to **OneDrive**, the online storage for that user.

Each user folder (including the **Public** folder) has a similar set of sub-folders defined.

If you don't see the full hierarchical structure of the user folders, right-click the Navigation pane and select **Expand to current folder**.

Show This PC
Show Network
Show libraries
Show all folders
Expand to current folder

The **Documents**, **Music**, **Pictures** and **Videos** sub-folders can be accessed from This PC in **File Explorer**, and also from the **Libraries** link that can be displayed on the Navigation pane (see page 104).

This PC

This PC in **File Explorer** is a feature that was added in Windows 10. Like the **Computer** option from previous versions of Windows, it provides a list of the storage devices and drives attached to the local computer.

 Open **File Explorer** and click **This PC**

 The lower group shows **Devices and drives**. In this example, there are two disk drives (**C:** and **D:**)

In addition, **File Explorer** lists some of the folders associated with the active user.

The upper group shows folders for the current user, including **Documents**, **Music**, **Pictures** and **Videos** (the same folders as used by **Libraries**)

The icons in Step 3 are shortcuts that link to the actual folders on the hard disk of the PC.

 The **Downloads** and **Desktop** folders are also listed in this group of folders

Cloud storage is a service in which data is stored on remote storage systems, where it is maintained, managed, backed up and made available to users over the internet. Users generally pay for cloud data storage at a monthly rate, although some services provide a limited amount for free.

Don't forget

When you view the **OneDrive** settings, you will see how much cloud storage you have, and how much of this is being used.

Hot tip

Only the folders you choose to sync will be shown in the local copy of **OneDrive**. Any changes you make are applied to the online **OneDrive** immediately, or the next time you connect to the internet.

OneDrive

OneDrive is Microsoft's cloud storage that comes with your Microsoft account. You can have up to 5GB storage free, and can access it from any device where you sign in with your Microsoft account, or from any web browser. **File Explorer** gives local copies of folders kept in sync with your **OneDrive**.

① Open **File Explorer** and select **OneDrive** > **Personal** in the Navigation pane to see the **OneDrive** folders that are kept locally

② You can also click the **OneDrive** icon in the **Notifications area** and select **Open folder** to open your OneDrive folder

③ To select files to sync, right-click the **OneDrive** icon, select **Settings**, then click **Choose folders** on the **Account** tab

There may be folders in your **OneDrive** not shown on the local copy. If you choose another folder, it will be added and its contents copied. If you deselect a folder, it and all of its files will be removed from the local copy.

...cont'd

4 Right-click the **OneDrive** icon and select **Upgrade** to see the options you have for getting additional storage

Open your OneDrive - Personal folder
Settings
View online
Unlock Personal Vault
Pause syncing
Upgrade
Get help
Send feedback
Close OneDrive

For up-to-date information on plan features, allowances and pricing, visit **onedrive.live.com/about/plans**

If you are signed in with a Local account, you may find **OneDrive** shown in **File Explorer**, but it will have no contents.

1 Select **OneDrive** from the Navigation pane, and you are invited to set up **OneDrive**

Set up OneDrive
Put your files in OneDrive to get them from any device.

Email address
[Enter your email address]

Create account   Sign in

You'll need a Microsoft account to complete the procedure.

Hot tip

By default, you get 5GB of free **OneDrive** storage space with Windows 11. Cloud storage is an excellent way to back up documents, since they are stored separately from your computer.

Beware

If you sign in with a Local account, the **OneDrive** entry may appear in **File Explorer**, but you cannot access OneDrive folders unless you provide a Microsoft account.

...cont'd

Using the OneDrive app

The **OneDrive** app can be used on a Windows 11 computer as another options for using the service. To do this:

 Download the **OneDrive** app from the Microsoft Store and click on this OneDrive

icon on the Start menu to open it. It should display the same items as in the **OneDrive** folder in **File Explorer**

 To add files to the **OneDrive** app, click on the **Upload** button

 Select whether to upload **Files** or a **Folder** from your computer

 Navigate to the required item in **File Explorer**, select it, and click on the **Select Folder** button to add it to your **OneDrive** folder

...cont'd

Using OneDrive online

It is also possible to view the contents of your **OneDrive**, and add to it, from the online version. To do this:

 To view the contents of **OneDrive** online, go to the website at **onedrive.live.com** and sign in with your Microsoft account details. Your **OneDrive** content is the same as in your **OneDrive** folder on your computer

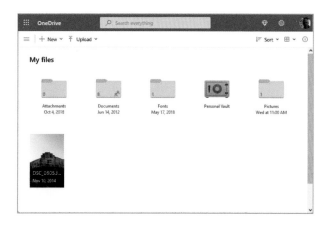

 Access your online **OneDrive** account and click on the **Upload** button

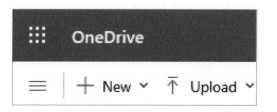

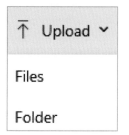 Select whether to upload **Files** or a **Folder** and navigate to the required items as on the previous page

Libraries

Libraries contain shortcuts to individual folders but allow you to treat the contents as if they were all in one folder. Typically, the **Documents** library would be a combination of the user's **Documents** folder and the **Public Documents** folder. This allows you to share documents with others (or access their documents). In Windows 11, libraries are not displayed by default, but you can add them to **File Explorer**.

1 Open **File Explorer** and right-click the Navigation pane, then select the **Show libraries** option

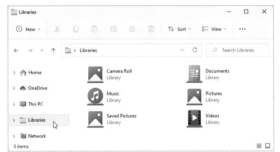

2 Select the **Libraries** entry that gets added, and you'll see the expected four libraries – **Documents**, **Pictures**, **Music** and **Videos** plus (perhaps) **Saved Pictures** and **Camera Roll**, used by the **Photos** and **Camera** apps

3 Double-click the **Documents** library and you'll see it has files from two locations – the user's OneDrive **Documents** folder (local copy of online folder) and the user's local **Documents** folder

Don't forget

Right-click any folder on your hard disk or OneDrive, select **Show more options** > **Include in library** and add it to any of your existing libraries, or use it to create a new library.

Folder navigation

When you open a drive or folder, you'll find a number of different ways to navigate around the folders on your disk.

1 Open, for example, a sub-folder in **Pictures** using **File Explorer**

Command bar   Menu bar   Search box   See more

Forward, Back

Up one level

Address bar

Navigation pane

Contents pane

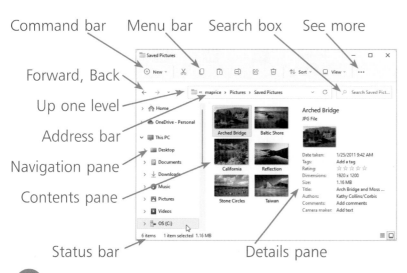

Status bar   Details pane

Click the **Forward** and **Back** arrows to navigate through locations you have already visited.

2 To go directly to a location on the **Address bar**, just click that location; for example, the user's folder (**maprice**, in this case)

3 To go to a sub-folder of a location on the **Address bar**, click the arrow to the right of that location, and select a sub-folder from the list displayed

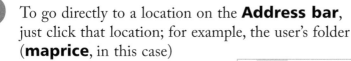

The **Address bar** displays the current location as a series of links, separated by arrows. There's an **Up** arrow at the left, to go up one level.

4 To type a location, click at the right of the **Address bar**

5 The full address for the current location is shown highlighted

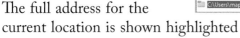

6 Press **Enter** to go to that location

For common locations, you can type just the name; for example:
- Computer
- Contacts
- Control Panel
- Documents
- Pictures

Creating folders and files

Hot tip

Create new folders to organize your documents by use or purpose, or create files of particular types, ready for use.

1 Open the library or folder where the new folder is required; e.g. select **This PC** > **Documents**

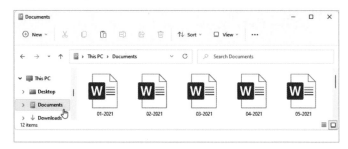

2 Right-click an empty part of the folder area and select **New** > **Folder**. Alternatively, you can select a specific file type

Don't forget

Choose one of the file types – for example, **Microsoft PowerPoint Presentation** – and it will be initially given the name **New Microsoft PowerPoint Presentation**. Rename it **Budget Plans**.

3 Overtype the name **New folder** with the required name, and press **Enter** (or click elsewhere)

If you create a folder or a file in a library, such as **Documents** or **Pictures**, it will be created and stored within the library's default save location; for example, the current user's **My Documents** or **My Pictures** folder.

Copying or moving files

You can copy one or more files using the Windows clipboard.

1 Open the folder containing the file, click the file icon to select it, and press **Ctrl + C**

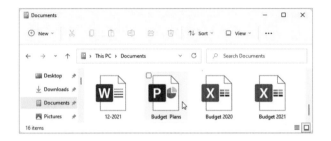

2 To copy multiple files, press the **Shift** or **Ctrl** keyboard keys and select all of the files before pressing **Ctrl + C**

3 Locate and open the destination folder, right-click an empty space and press **Ctrl + V** to create a copy of the file in that folder

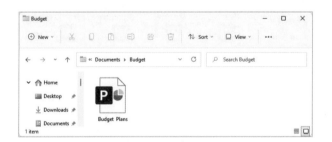

4 To move a file to a new location rather than make a copy, right-click the file icon and press **Ctrl + X**

5 The original file icon will be grayed out until you press **Ctrl + V** at the new location, and it will be moved there

Budget 2021

Hot tip

You can right-click the file icon and select **Show more options** > **Copy**, to copy a file to the clipboard.

| Cut |
| Copy |
| Create shortcut |

Hot tip

Also, right-click a folder and select **Show more options** > **Paste**, to copy a file from the clipboard.

| Paste |
| Paste shortcut |
| Undo Delete   Ctrl+Z |

Hot tip

Alternatively, right-click a file icon and select **Show more options** > **Cut** to initiate moving a file.

| Cut |
| Copy |
| Create shortcut |

...cont'd

To move or copy files using drag and drop operations:

 1 Use **File Explorer** to locate and open the folder containing files you want to move

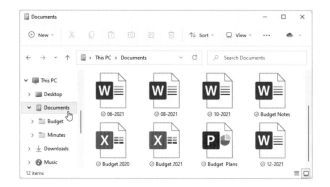

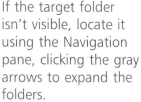
 2 Select a first file then press the **Ctrl** key as you select a second and subsequent files

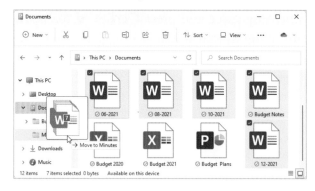

| Copy here |
| **Move here** |
| Create shortcuts here |
| Cancel |

 3 Click and hold any of the selected files, then drag the selection to the target folder and release there

 4 To copy rather than move the selected files, hold down **Ctrl** as you drag and release the selection

> **+ Copy to Minutes**

5 If the target folder is in a different drive, hold down **Shift** as you drag to move – otherwise, you will copy

Deleting files

To remove files from a folder:

1 Select a file or files, and either right-click the selection and choose the **Delete** command or press the keyboard **Delete** key

2 If the file is located anywhere other than your hard disk, you are asked to confirm permanent deletion

3 Files on the hard disk are moved to the **Recycle Bin**, usually with the warning message turned off

To recover a file deleted by mistake:

1 Right-click the **Recycle Bin** icon and select **Open** (or just double-click the icon)

2 Select a file or files you want to be recovered

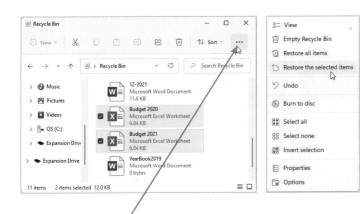

3 Click **See more**, and then **Restore the selected items**

4 The files are returned to their original locations

Hot tip

The **Recycle Bin** can be accessed by double-clicking on its icon on the desktop.

Don't forget

To remove hard disk files completely without using the **Recycle Bin** as an interim store, hold down **Shift** as you select **Delete**. You'll be asked to confirm. The deleted files then cannot be recovered.

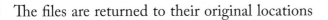

File Explorer no longer displays the **Ribbon** that featured in previous releases of Windows.

Don't forget

From the **View** options you can choose **Compact view** to decrease space between items and get to see more of the entries at once.

Folder views

File Explorer offers a variety of ways to view file and sub-folder entries that are contained in your folders and libraries. For example:

1 Open a library or folder, such as **Saved Pictures**, and note the file list style used (in this case, **Large icons**)

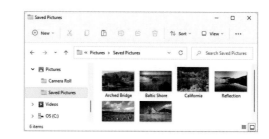

2 Right-click an empty part of the folder area and select **View**, to see the various styles, with the current setting identified by a bullet

3 Choose any of the four icon sizes offered to see how the folder contents are displayed

Extra large icons   Large icons

Medium icons   Small icons

Other views can offer extra information about files.

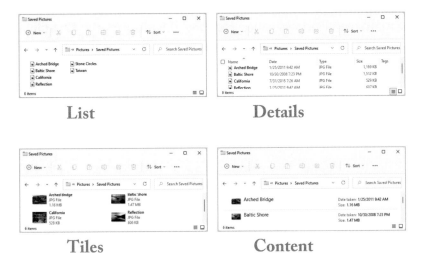

List   Details

Tiles   Content

A file-type icon rather than a thumbnail is used for **Small icons**, **List** and **Details** views.

The details provided with the **Content** view depend on the file type, and on the data provided when the file was created.

The options in the **Sort** menu also depend on the type of file for which the folder has been optimized. To illustrate:

The options in the sub-menus (**More** and **Group by**) will also be determined by the folder type.

Documents	Music	Videos	Downloads
• Name	• Name	• Name	Name
Status	#	Date	• Date modified
Date modified	Title	Type	Type
More >	More >	More >	More >
• Ascending	• Ascending	• Ascending	Ascending
Descending	Descending	Descending	• Descending
Group by >	Group by >	Group by >	Group by >

Documents Music Videos Downloads

Home folder

To help you search for apps and to quickly access the ones you use frequently, Windows 11 has a directory within **File Explorer** windows called **Home**. This displays the **Quick access** and **Favorites** sections, where various files and folders can be added. To use the **Home** folder:

The **Home** folder and **Quick access** have been updated in Windows 11.

1 Open **File Explorer** and by default it will display the **Home** folder, consisting of **Quick access**, **Favorites** and **Recent**

2 Select **View > Show** and click the **Navigation pane** option

3 The **Home** folders are now displayed with the Navigation pane hidden

To add items to the **Home** folder:

1 Right-click a folder and select **Pin to Quick access**. The folder you select will appear in

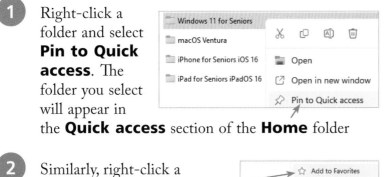

the **Quick access** section of the **Home** folder

2 Similarly, right-click a file and choose **Add to Favorites**, and it is added to the Pinned files section

To show or hide the **Recents** section in the **Home** folder:

1 In **File Explorer**, click **See more (...)** and select **Options** to display the **Folder Options** panel

2 Select the **General** tab and choose **Open File Explorer to: > Home**

3 Click the **Show recently used files** and **Show frequently used folders** options (getting checkmarks in the boxes), then click **OK**

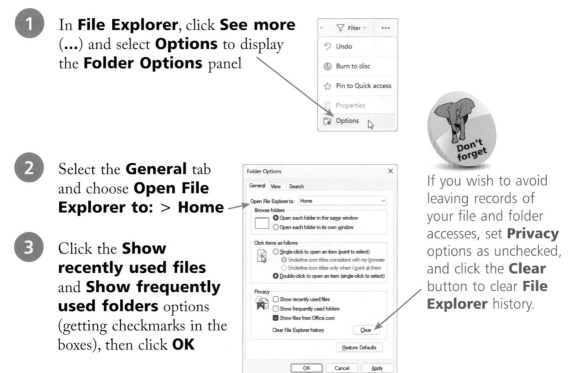

Don't forget

To remove folders and files from the Home folder: for **Quick access** folders, right-click on the folder and select **Unpin from Quick access**; for **Favorites** files, right-click on the file and select **Unpin from Favorites**.

Don't forget

If you wish to avoid leaving records of your file and folder accesses, set **Privacy** options as unchecked, and click the **Clear** button to clear **File Explorer** history.

113

Windows Search

Windows offers a variety of methods of initiating a search for a file or folders.

1 Press the **WinKey** + **S** key combination to display the **Search** panel

You can also display the **Search** panel by holding the cursor over the **Search** icon on the Taskbar, and then clicking the **Select here to search** entry.

2 Begin typing your search request, and matches for the text are listed as you type

3 Press **Enter** if the **Best match** meets your need, or select one of the apps listed

...cont'd

You can also initiate searches for files and folders from the Start menu.

1 Press **WinKey** or click the **Start** button on the Taskbar

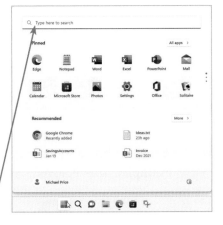

Don't forget

Click the **Power** button, which is on the lower right of the Start menu, to display the **Shut down/ Restart** menu.

⚙ Sign-in options

☾ Sleep

⟳ Update and shut down

⏻ Shut down

↻ Update and restart

↺ Restart

2 Click in the **Type here to search** box, and the Search panel will be displayed

3 Click the arrow (**>**) next to a setting, to open that setting or to access its functions

4 Click **See web results** to display a list of related topics that are available on the internet

Search the web

🔍 cal - See web results >

Hot tip

Just click on the name to run an app or to open a setting.

📅 Calendar >

Search box

If you want to access a file but are not sure which sub-folder it is in, you can start at the higher-level folder and use the **Search** box to find the exact location.

1 Open **File Explorer** at **This PC**, the highest level

Hot tip

You don't have to worry about using capital letters in your search text, since the case and the word sequence are ignored.

Hot tip

You can click the **Start Search** button after each word and see how many references you find as the search expression builds.

2 Click in the **Search** box and start typing the search words – for example: "this is love"

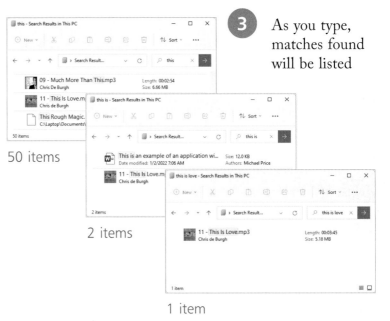

3 As you type, matches found will be listed

50 items

2 items

1 item

Don't forget

At any stage, if you detect the required file in the list of results, double-click it to open it.

4 Stop typing when the results show the file you are seeking, or complete your search request to get the most compact list of references

In the above example, the initial results included documents and songs, while the final result was a single song.

6 Classic applications

Windows 11 includes some useful Classic apps for doing calculations, word processing and picture editing.

These applications take advantage of Windows 11 features and can be pinned to the Start menu.

About Classic applications

Windows 11 provides the operating environment for a variety of applications. In many cases, these are supplied as separate programs or suites of programs. However, some of the desired functions may be in the form of small but potentially very useful programs in the **Windows Accessories** and **Windows Tools** folders (see below). The main application areas and the included Windows programs are:

- Text processing: **Sticky Notes**, **Notepad**.
- Word processing: **WordPad**.
- Electronic mail: **Windows Fax and Scan**.
- Drawing: **Paint**.
- Spreadsheet: **Math Recognizer**.
- Database: **Character Map**, **Steps Recorder**.
- Multimedia: **Snipping Tool**, **XPS Viewer**.

To see which applications are available:

 Right-click **Start**, select **Run** and type the command *%ProgramData%\microsoft\windows\Start menu\Programs* then select **OK**

The **Programs** folder is displayed, with links to the **Windows Accessories** folder and the **Windows Tools** folder.

For functions that are not provided by the programs included with Windows, you'll need to install programs such as **Adobe Acrobat** or **Microsoft Office**, or make use of free readers and viewers, for specific file and document types.

Notepad

Notepad is a text editor that you can use to create, view or modify text (**.txt**) files. It provides only very basic formatting, and handles text a line at a time.

 Locate **Notepad** in the **All apps** list, click to open, then type some text, pressing **Enter** for each new line

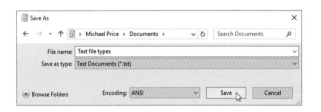

 Select **File** > **Save As** and type the required file name (with **.txt** file type), then click **Save**

 If the text is longer than the window width, select **View** > **Word wrap**, to fit the text within the window

When you print the file, it will wrap according to the paper width, regardless of the word-wrap setting

Don't forget

The absence of formatting turns into a benefit when you are working with the source files for a program or the HTML code for a web page, since these require pure text.

Hot tip

Click **Edit** > **Go To...** and then type a line number to go to that specific line in the file (as will be indicated on the Status bar).

119

WordPad

WordPad also offers text editing, but adds tools and facilities for more complex formatting of individual pieces of text.

1 Start **WordPad** from **Windows Tools** in **All apps** or from the **Windows Accessories** folder, and type text, pressing **Enter** for each new paragraph

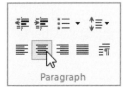
2 Use the **Formatting bar** to change the font, size, style and color for selected (highlighted) text

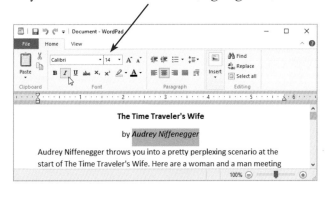

3 Click the **Save** button on the **Quick access** toolbar (or press **Ctrl + S**) to save the document

...cont'd

Inserting pictures

WordPad also allows you to include pictures in documents.

1 Position the typing cursor and click **Insert** then the **Picture** button on the **Home** tab

2 Locate and select a picture, then click **Open**

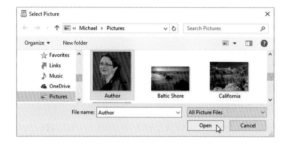

You can also click the **Paint drawing** button to insert a drawing that you create using **Paint** (see pages 122-123).

3 A copy of the image is added to the document and displayed at the cursor location

4 If it's the wrong size, right-click the picture and select **Resize picture**

5 Choose the scale factor you desire, usually keeping the same aspect ratio, and click **OK** to resize

Paint

Paint is used to draw, edit and color images that you create from scratch, or to modify digital photos or web page graphics. There is also a **Paint 3D** app designed to create and modify 3D objects.

To create a picture in **Paint** from an existing image file:

1 Select **Paint** from the **All apps** list, and it starts up with a blank canvas

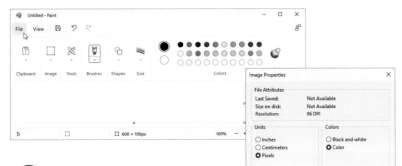

2 Select **File** > **Image Properties** to reset the canvas size to 800 x 500 pixels and click **OK** to apply the change

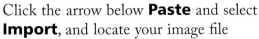

3 Click the arrow below **Paste** and select **Import**, and locate your image file

4 Click **Open** to add the picture

5 Drag the image to position it centrally, with space for a title

If the pasted image is larger than the canvas, the canvas will automatically be extended to hold the picture.

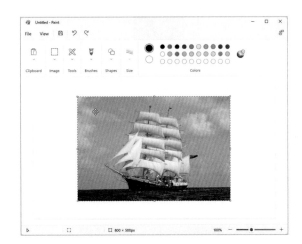

Click **Shapes**, select the **Rounded rectangle** tool, then click and drag to draw a frame around the picture

Hot tip

For a more realistic effect, draw a second frame outside the first and use the **Fill** tool to color the space between the frames.

123

7 Use the **Text** tool to draw text boxes and add information such as a picture title and a description of the contents

8 To make editing easier, drag the slider (or click **+**) to zoom in on the window

Don't forget

Choose a suitable file type such as **.tiff** for pictures, or **.png** for documents. Paint also supports **.bmp**, **.gif** and **.jpeg** file formats.

9 When you finish the additions, select **File** > **Save As**, choose a type, enter a file name and click **Save**

Unknown file types

Windows and its applications cannot help when you receive attachments or download files of unknown file types, but it will do its best to search for alternative options.

1 If there are unknown file types in your current folder, the extensions are displayed

2 Right-click an unknown file type – **HTM file**, for example – and select **Open with**

3 Select an app to open the file; e.g. **Microsoft Edge** for HTM files. If none is suitable, select **Look for an app in the Microsoft Store** and click **OK**

4 There may be many apps offered, some free and some chargeable, so you'll have to pick out the one you think most suitable

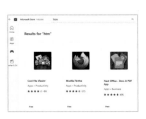

Changing the default app

It is possible to change the default apps that are used to open specific file types. To do this (for a text **.odt** file):

1 Right-click any **.odt** file and select **Open with**

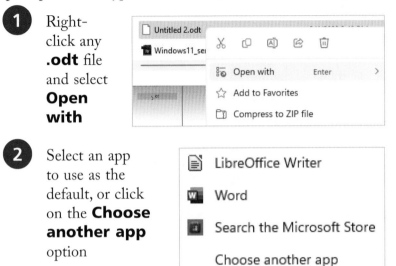

2 Select an app to use as the default, or click on the **Choose another app** option

- LibreOffice Writer
- Word
- Search the Microsoft Store
- Choose another app

3 In this case, **Word** is shown as default for **.odt** files (which is a text document format)

How do you want to open this file?

- LibreOffice Writer
- Word
- Look for an app in the Microsoft Store

More apps ↓

☑ Always use this app to open .odt files

OK

4 Select another option, and click the **Always use this app** box, if you want it as the new default

5 Click **OK** to apply the new selection

Hot tip

You can review and change the default app that is associated with any particular file type.

Hot tip

Select the **Search the Microsoft Store** option in Step 2 to find other apps that can open document files.

...cont'd

The file icon indicates the file type and helps identify which application opens when you double-click that icon.

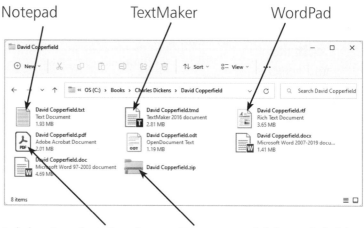

Notepad   TextMaker   WordPad

Adobe Acrobat Reader   Compressed (zipped) folder

If you have **Microsoft Word** installed, as an application or as part of Microsoft Office, you'll find that it can open and save files in a number of different formats.

To see the formats that it supports, open a text file in Word and select **File** > **Save As**. Choose a **Save** location and then click in the **Save as type:** box.

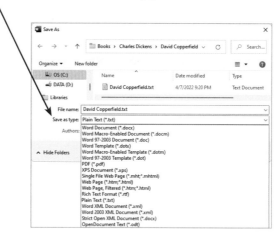

Choose the format you desire and click the **Save** button to complete the action.

You are offered various Word-related formats, several Web Page formats and a number of specialized document formats.

7 Universal apps

The emphasis is now on Universal apps in Windows 11. Some are supplied at installation and there are also many Universal apps in the Microsoft Store, where you can search, review descriptions, then download and install apps on your system, for a variety of uses.

In the past, Windows applications have been available from many sources, including supplier and enthusiast websites, as well as Microsoft. Sources for Windows apps are now much more limited.

All Universal apps must be submitted to Microsoft for certification before they are allowed in the Microsoft Store (or included on installation discs).

Sources for apps

Although Windows Classic applications are supported, the main functions are provided by Universal apps in Windows 11. As already discussed, these can run full-screen or windowed, and can use Windows **Snap Layouts** to allow two or more apps to share the screen.

The primary design point for the Universal app is the touchscreen, as exemplified by the tablet PC, but all the apps can also be operated on a system with standard monitor, mouse and keyboard equipment.

The Windows apps that are available can be found in just two places:

● Supplied and installed with Windows 11.

This is a typical Start menu for a Windows 11 system, showing some of the Windows apps you may expect to find pinned to the Start menu.

● Via the Microsoft Store, where you find ranges of free apps and paid apps to download and install.

The variety of Universal apps available at the Microsoft Store will change frequently, as new products are added and existing products are revised or removed.

Programs submitted to Microsoft can also include Classic apps. These are conventional applications that are listed in the Microsoft Store, but provided from the manufacturer's website via a link that is included with the application description. These, and other conventional apps, may still be obtained directly, without visiting the Microsoft Store.

Supplied with Windows 11

To see which apps have been installed on your system:

 1 Select **Settings** > **Apps**

Don't forget

Another way to list all the apps on your system is to left-click the **Start** button and then click the **All apps** button.

All the apps will be listed, and this list will be preceded by a list of **Most used** apps.

2 Select **Installed apps** to list your apps

In this example there are 80 apps, and these are listed alphabetically. Drag the scroll bar or rotate the scroll wheel on your mouse to see all the apps that are provided.

On the following pages, we will look at the **Calculator**, **Clock** and **Weather** apps. We also review the Microsoft Store and the app categories that it offers, and discuss the Search option that helps you locate apps related to specific topics.

Other apps, such as **Mail**, **Calendar**, **Microsoft Edge**, **Photos** and the various games apps, will be discussed in the relevant chapters on the specific topics.

Hot tip

You can pin any of these apps onto the Start menu so that they appear in the **Pinned** area.

Calculator

While it is no substitute for a full spreadsheet application, the Windows **Calculator** app provides quite powerful computational facilities.

 Select the **Calculator** app from the **All apps** list on the Start menu

 In **Standard** mode, type or click to enter a calculation using the desired operation symbol, and press = to display the result

Click the function buttons or press the equivalent keyboard keys, to perform add, subtract, multiply, divide, square root, percentage and inverse operations. You can also store and recall numbers from memory, and the **History** capability keeps track of stages in the calculations.

In addition to the **Standard** mode, there are also **Scientific** and **Programmer** modes, plus a variety of **Converter** options provided.

 Open **Calculator**, then click the **Menu** button to list the modes

 Select **Scientific** to see the features it offers

Scientific mode gives a variety of logarithmic, trigonometric and factorial functions in various forms, such as degrees, radians etc.

3 Select **Programmer** mode to see what it has to offer

The **Programmer** calculator operates in decimal, hexadecimal, octal and binary formats. It supports byte, word, dword and qword. There's a full keypad, including alphabetics for hex numbers, and an alternative bit-toggling keypad.

Unlike the other **Calculator** modes, **Programmer** mode does not maintain a history of computations.

There are 13 different **Converter** options, each with a range of units.

 4 Select the **Converter** mode, and select a category – for example, **Weight and mass** – and choose **From** and **To** units; e.g. **Kilograms** to **Pounds**

Note how the converter suggests some equivalents, in related units – in this example, the number of soccer balls.

Each of the categories offers a range of appropriate units, and they all suggest equivalents to your results, sometimes quite idiosyncratic in nature.

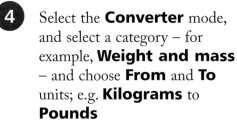

 5 Switch to the **Energy** category to convert between **Food calories** and **Kilojoules**

6 Enter 2500 as the starting value

You are told that this quantity of energy is about equal to 9,914 BTUs (British Thermal Units) or 9.99 slices of cake!

The **Weight and mass** category offers a total of 14 different units that you can convert to and from.

Clock

The **Clock** app is a combination of **World Clock**, **Alarm Clock**, **Stopwatch** and **Timer**. You can use it to set alarms and reminders, to check the time anywhere in the world, and to time your activities.

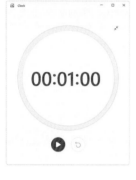
1 Select **Clock** from **All apps** and click the **Menu** button

2 Select any of the four types of clock to review its features

3 Select **Focus sessions** to deal with specific tasks. This integrates with the **Microsoft To Do** app and with **Spotify** and includes automatic breaks

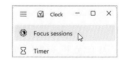

Weather

This app displays forecasts of temperature, wind direction and speed, humidity etc. for your default or chosen location.

1 Select **Weather** from the Start menu to see an overview for the current day

2 Choose a later date if desired, then view the forecast, selecting either **Summary** or **Details**

3 Scroll down in either view to see details for the specified day, including historical peaks and averages

The **Weather** app runs on other devices such as tablets and smartphones, and adjusts itself to suit their particular screen sizes.

Click the buttons on the **Icon bar** to display maps, historical weather or favorite locations. Click the **Menu** button to show the titles of icons.

Microsoft Store

The **Microsoft Store** recognizes which version of Windows your system is running and displays apps appropriate for you. To see what's offered:

The **Microsoft Store** is the source for new Universal apps for your Windows 11 system, and is organized to help you identify useful items.

 Touch or click the **Microsoft Store** icon on the Start menu or on the Taskbar to open the Store at the homepage

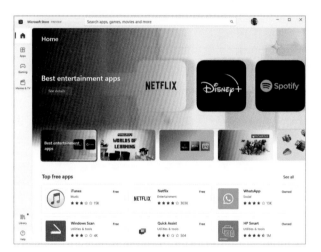

The **Microsoft Store** can display all types of items with **Home** selected, or you can restrict it to **Apps**, **Gaming** or **Movies & TV** (**Films & TV** in some regions) items.

 You will see several highlighted apps and a selection of **Top free** apps

 Scroll down to the entry; e.g. **Music streaming apps**

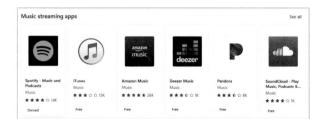

 Click the **See all** link alongside the group name to display all items in the group

See all

...cont'd

All apps in the group are made available for display.

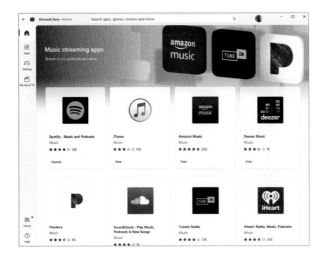

Scroll down to display any other items in the group.

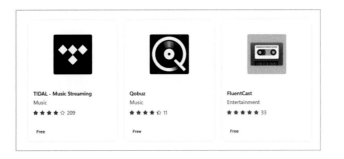

The entry for each app shows whether it is already installed or available for download – either free of charge or at a price.

The price stated will be in the currency appropriate to your location; e.g. Dollars for the US, and Sterling for the UK.

Hot tip

Items in the **Microsoft Store** are arranged in various groupings, to help you find things that are useful to you. For example, apps are grouped as:

- **Top free**
- **Essential**
- **Entertainment**
- **Productivity**
- **Creativity**
- **New & trending**
- **Top paid**
- **Specials**
- **Collections**

Collections

The **Collections** section can be accessed from the **Apps** homepage in the Microsoft Store and includes:

Creativity apps
This collection holds a total of 34 apps, most of which are provided at no charge.

Select the **See all** button at the right-hand side of the main **Collections** window to list all collections offered by the Microsoft Store.

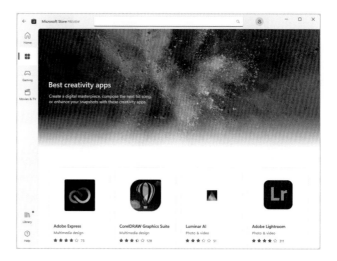

Apps for developing young minds
There are 29 apps in this collection, more than half of which are provided free of charge, while the remainder can be purchased at a relatively low price.

Searching the Microsoft Store

You can use the Search box found on the Microsoft Store screen to view its scope and find items of interest.

 Select the Search box and type a search term – for example, "aquatic"

 The top few matches are displayed immediately

 Click the magnifying glass icon to show all the results

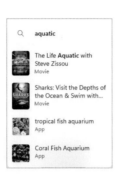

Don't forget

You may not be sure of the exact name of the app you need, but you can search the Microsoft Store using a descriptive term, to identify the app.

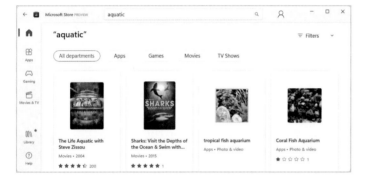

You'll be shown results for all departments, and you can then choose to view an individual grouping – **Apps**, **Games**, **Movies** or **TV Shows**.

 Select the **Apps** button to list all apps related to your search term

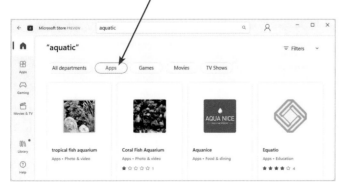

Installing apps

Don't forget

If you already own this app, you'll see the **Install** button (or **Launch** button, if already installed) rather than the **Get** button.

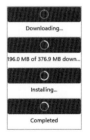

Hot tip

During the process, messages from the Microsoft Store let you know the progress of actions being performed.

 1 Find an app you want to investigate; for example, **Adobe Acrobat Reader**

Adobe Acrobat Reader DC
Apps • Productivity
★★★★☆ 237

 2 If you decide you want this app on your system, click the **Get** button

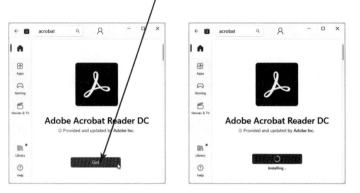

 3 The app is downloaded and installed

 4 You will find an entry for the app in the **All apps** list

Adobe Acrobat DC
New

5 Right-click the **All apps** entry and select **Pin to Start** to add it to the Pinned section of the Start menu

Pinned

Notepad   Adobe Acrobat DC

6 Select either entry for **Adobe Acrobat Reader** to launch the application

Your Microsoft account

From the Microsoft Store, you can go to your Microsoft account to list the devices and apps that have been installed for this account.

 Open the **Microsoft Store** app and click the **Profile** button, then select **Manage account and devices**

 Microsoft Edge opens the web page for your Microsoft account

 Scroll down to display the devices that are associated with this account

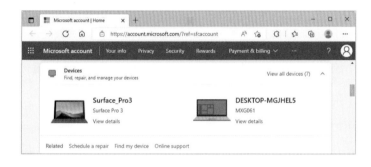

 Scroll on down to access further details of your Microsoft account

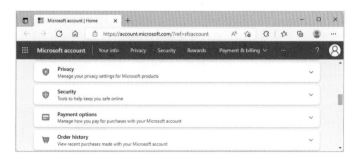

You can review your privacy settings, access security tools, manage payment options and review the order history for your Microsoft account.

Don't forget

You can choose to personalize the account by adding a profile photo that will appear on apps and devices that use the Microsoft account.

Beware

You can install apps from the Store, free or charged, on up to 10 Windows 11 devices, including PCs, tablets, smartphones and gaming devices, all associated with the same Microsoft account, although you are limited to four devices for the **Music** and **Video** apps.

Updates

If any Universal app that you've installed gets updated, the changes are supplied through the Microsoft Store. In Windows 11, these updates are applied automatically in the background, without any notification by default.

If you'd prefer to manually accept and install updates:

1 Open **Microsoft Store**, click the **Profile** icon and select **App settings**

2 Click the button for **App updates**, to turn off automatic updating

When you drag an option button, it will change color from the accent color (**On**) to white (**Off**) or vice versa, to indicate the changed status.

3 The setting for **App updates** is reversed

4 To view the update status, select **Library** from the Icon bar on the **App settings** panel, to find a count and list of **Updates & downloads**

...cont'd

Scroll on down to see a full list of items for your account. These can include **Apps**, **Games** and **Movies & TV**.

Don't forget

Items may be flagged with a cloud icon. This means that the item is available online but is not currently installed on your device. Click the icon to initiate the installation.

Select a group – **Games**, for example – to list its contents.

Select any of the entries listed, to check its status on the current device.

Hot tip

If you already own a game but it's not present on the current device, you'll see an Install button. If the game is installed, you'll see a **Play** button.

Verifying your identity

It is possible to verify your Microsoft account so that details from it can be synchronized online and across different devices for the same account. To do this:

 Open the **Settings** app and click on the **Accounts** category in the left-hand sidebar

| Accounts

Click on the **Your info** option

Account settings

℞ Your info
Profile photo

 Click on the **Verify** button

Account settings

ⓘ Verify your identity to sync passwords across your devices.   Verify

Don't forget

You can select either an email address or a telephone number, depending what contact information is in the profile for your Microsoft account.

4 Click on the email address used for the Microsoft account. An email will be sent to this account

▮▮ Microsoft

nickvandome@gmail.com

Verify your identity

✉ Email nickvandome@gmail.com

I have a code

Show more verification methods

Cancel

5 Enter the code sent in the email and click on the **Verify** button to verify your Microsoft account

▮▮ Microsoft

← nickvandome@gmail.com

Enter code

✉ We emailed a code to nickvandome@gmail.com. Please enter the code to sign in.

Code

Verify

Authenticator app

The **Microsoft Authenticator** app can be used if you need to verify your Microsoft account when you are logging in to it. This can be done from a mobile device, such as a tablet or a smartphone, giving an additional layer of security. It can also be used to access non-Microsoft accounts online. To obtain and use the app:

 Visit the app store for your mobile device; an iPad, for example

 Search the app store for "microsoft authenticator"

This illustrates adding the **Microsoft Authenticator** app for the iPad. A similar process will be needed to add the equivalent app for your smartphone.

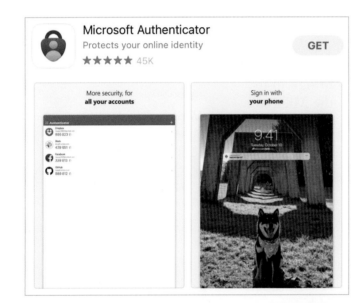

 Select **Get** and then select **Install** for the **Microsoft Authenticator** app, to add it to your mobile device

 Tap on the **Microsoft Authenticator** app on your mobile device to open it

...cont'd

The app is now ready for you to add the Microsoft accounts you may need to verify.

 1 Click **Add account** and to start validating your Microsoft account

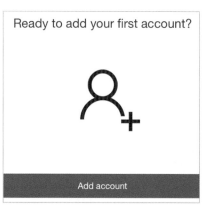

Ready to add your first account?

Add account

Hot tip

You can be added as a new user to any Windows 11 device, and use your Microsoft account to sign in to that device.

 2 Follow prompts to sign in to the Microsoft account and click on the email address used for the account

Microsoft

nickvandome@mac.com

Verify your identity

✉ Email nickvandome@mac.com

I have a code

I don't have any of these

Cancel

Hot tip

The next time you need to verify your identity, it will call upon the **Microsoft Authenticator** app, and you can approve the request on your mobile device.

3 A verification code is sent to the email address selected in Step 2. Enter this in the authenticator and tap on the **Verify** button

Microsoft

← nickvandome@mac.com

Enter code

✉ We emailed a code to nickvandome@mac.com. Please enter the code to sign in.

Code

Cancel   Verify

144

8 Email and more

Windows 11 provides the Mail app for email communications, the People app to manage your contacts, and the Calendar app to keep track of events and appointments. The Chat app can also be used for video chats.

An email address consists of a username or nickname, the @ sign, and the server name of your email provider – e.g. *jsmith99@myisp.com* – or web service – e.g. *jsmith99@gmail.com*

You can access instant messaging (and make video and phone calls) using **Chat**, which is part of the **Microsoft Teams** app (see pages 158-161) to get started.

Electronic mail

Email or electronic mail is used to send and receive digital messages. You can send an email message to anyone with an email address, you can receive messages from anyone who knows your email address, and you can reply to those messages or forward them to another email address. You can send your email message to more than one person at the same time and attach files such as documents or pictures.

Email is free, since no stamp or fee is required. However, before you can use email, you require:

- An account with an Internet Service Provider (ISP).

- An internet connection such as telephone or cable.

- A modem or router to make the connection.

- An email address from your email service provider or from a web service such as **Gmail** or **Hotmail**.

- An email program such as **Mail** or **Outlook**.

Mail

This is the Windows app that is installed along with **Calendar** when Windows 11 is set up. It provides full-screen access to multiple email accounts.

Outlook

This application is included in all editions of **Microsoft Office** except the Home & Student edition, and is installed with Windows 11 systems that have **Office** added. It provides fully functioning email and time management services, and runs on the desktop as a windowed application.

Other email programs

There are many other apps in the Microsoft Store that supplement the features of the **Mail** app. For example, **Email Backgrounds** provides colorful email stationery.

Windows 11 Mail app

To get started with the **Mail** app:

1 On the **Start** menu select the tile for the **Mail** app, or do this from the Taskbar

2 The **Mail** app is launched

3 **Mail** identifies your Microsoft account as Outlook.com, ready for you to select, if required

Office has a new look ✕

Welcome to the newly refreshed Office. We've made some changes we think will help you focus more on your work.

1 of 3

Learn more

Show me   Not now

Hot tip

To add another email account when there are existing accounts, the **Add account** option in Step 4 is used too.

4 **Mail** shows any accounts you may have already added. If there's no existing email account, click on the **Add account** option

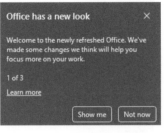

Manage accounts

Select an account to edit settings.

🔗 Link inboxes

+ Add account

5 Select your account type – for example, **Gmail** – enter your email address and then click **Next**

Add an account ✕

Suggested

G nickvandome@gmail.com
    Google

Outlook.com
Outlook.com, Live.com, Hotmail, MSN

Create Free Account
Get a free personal Outlook email address

Office 365
Office 365, Exchange

G Google

Yahoo!

iCloud

Other account
POP, IMAP

⚙ Advanced setup

6 Enter the password for your email account and then click **Next**

7 Click **Done** when the account has been added successfully

Sign in
to continue to Windows

Email or phone

Forgot email?

To continue, Google will share your name, email address, language preference and profile picture with Windows. Before using this app, you can review Windows's privacy policy and Terms of Service.

Create account   Next

...cont'd

Hot tip

If you have multiple email accounts, click the **Accounts** button to change accounts.

Accounts

When **Mail** starts up, the display layout that you see depends on the screen resolution. On a higher-resolution monitor – in this case, 1280 x 1024 pixels – you'll see the expanded **Icon bar** and the **Current Folder** and **Reading** panes.

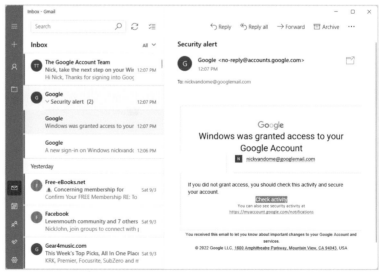

Don't forget

Click the **Expand/ Collapse** button on the **Icon bar** to display the titles for icons, and list accounts and folders.

On a lower-resolution monitor (the example below is just 1024 x 768 pixels) you'll see only two folders – the **Current Folder** and **Reading** panes, plus the **Icon bar**.

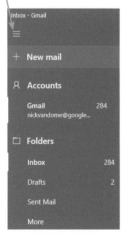

Mail app settings

1 Click **Settings** on the **Icon bar** to show all the options

2 Select **Manage accounts** to choose an account and edit its settings

3 Click **Add account** if you want to define another email account to use with the **Mail** app

Settings

Manage accounts
Personalization
Automatic replies
Focused inbox
Message list
Reading pane
Signature
Default Font
Notifications
Email security
What's new
Outlook for Android and iOS
Help
Trust Center
Feedback
Experiment
About

< Manage accounts

Select an account to edit settings.

✉ Gmail
nickvandome@googlemail.com

⊘ Link inboxes

+ Add account

< Personalization

Preview

Colors

Use my Windows accent color

○ Light mode
○ Dark mode
● Use my Windows mode

4 Select **Personalization** to select an image for the **Reading** pane, displayed when no message is selected

Email signature

Select an account and customize your signature

Gmail

☐ Apply to all accounts

Use an email signature

⬤ On

B *I* U A Calibri (Body) 11 ✎ ▥

Sent from Mail for Windows.

Save   Cancel

5 Select **Signature** to specify a default email signature to be appended to the messages you send from a specific account, or from all accounts

< Notifications

Notification settings can be customized for each of your accounts.

Select an account

Gmail

☐ Apply to all accounts

Show notifications in the action center

⬤ On

☑ Show a notification banner

☐ Play a sound

☐ Show notifications for folders pinned to Start

6 Select **Notifications** to customize the notification settings, again for a specific account or for all of your accounts

7 Select other entries in the **Settings** list to see which of them apply to your particular system

Quick Action icons for **Archive**, **Delete** and **Flag** are displayed when you move the mouse pointer over a message in the Inbox.

⊟ 🗑 ⚑

The Mail window

These are the main elements of the **Mail** window:

Accounts

Selected account

Selected message

Selected folder

Folder list

Mailbox folder

Reading pane

Respond

Delete

More options

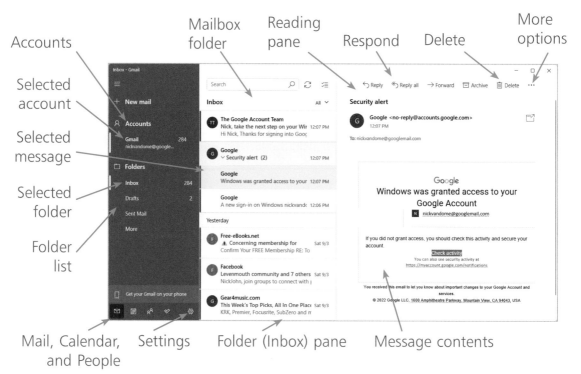

Mail, Calendar, and People

Settings

Folder (Inbox) pane

Message contents

Hot tip

The **Mail** tile on the Start menu displays the message count and message extracts (even if **Mail** is closed). The message count may also appear on the Taskbar icon.

1. Click **More options (...)** at the top right of the window to display commands for dealing with the messages in your Mailbox

2. Click the **Zoom** button to list the scale factors offered

3. Click the arrow at the top of the Zoom list to return to the options list. Click anywhere on the **Mail** window away from the lists to remove them

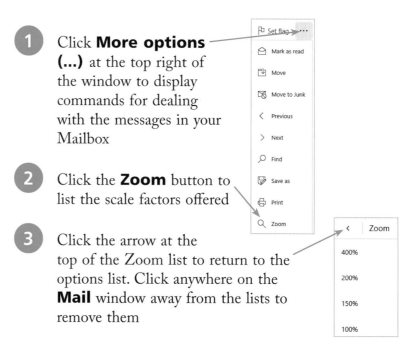

Viewing messages

1 Select a message from the **Folder** pane and it displays in the **Reading** pane

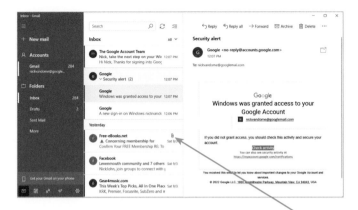

Pictures can be included in the body of email messages, as well as saved from them. Other files such as documents can also be sent, saved or opened from a message.

2 If there is an attachment (as indicated by a paperclip icon) it will be contained within the email body or shown as a link

3 Click **Reply** to respond to the sender, **Reply all** for all addressees, or **Forward** to send to another person

You can add recipients from your **Contacts** list (see pages 154-155).

4 Type your reply and click the **Send** button when finished

5 A copy is saved in the **Sent** folder of the account used to send the reply

Creating a message

1 In **Mail**, select an email account, go to the Inbox and click the **New mail** button (or press **Ctrl + N**)

2 A blank message is displayed, ready for recipient details and content

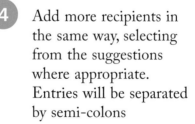

Don't forget

When entering contact names in the **To:** box, you may see several suggestions that match so far, but the number reduces as you enter more of the name.

3 Begin typing a contact name in the **To:** box, then select the contact when it appears in the results below

4 Add more recipients in the same way, selecting from the suggestions where appropriate. Entries will be separated by semi-colons

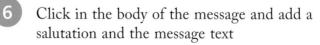

Hot tip

To attach an item to an email, click the **Insert** tab in Step 4. Choose an option from the **Insert** toolbar, which includes **File**, **Table**, **Pictures**, **Link**, and **Emoji**.

5 Click in the **Subject** box and type text for the title of the message

6 Click in the body of the message and add a salutation and the message text

7 End with your name, then the email signature for the sending account will be added automatically, if you have this set up (see page 149)

8 Select **Cc & Bcc** to add boxes for recipients who will be copied on the email

9 You can format the text in your message if you wish – click the **Styles** button to see more options

Format	Insert	Draw	⌄

A ｜ ≡¶ | Heading 1 ⌄

Styles

Normal

No Spacing

Heading 1

Heading 2

Hot tip

Recipients added using **Bcc** (Blind carbon-copy) will not be shown on copies of the message that others receive.

10 There are also font formatting and paragraph formatting options

Format	**Insert**	Draw	⌄	🗑 Discard

| 📎 Files | ▦ Table | 🖼 Pictures | 🔗 Link | ☺ Emoji |

Don't forget

Sometimes a message to an email address may fail, perhaps because the domain server is offline for a period. After several attempts, an error response message may be returned to you.

11 Click the **Send** button to send the message

▷ Send

153

If the **People** app is being used for the first time there will be a page with an option to add contacts from an existing account, such as **Google** or **iCloud**. If an account has already been added for the **Mail** app then this can be used, and there is also an **Import contacts** option for importing from another account.

Hot tip

You can also select accounts to add to the **People** app from the homepage when you first open it.

Hot tip

To delete a contact, right-click on their name in the **Contacts** list and click on the **Delete** button to remove it.

People

An electronic address book is always a good feature to have on a computer, and with Windows 11 this function is provided by the **People** app. This not only allows you to add your own contacts manually; you can also link to any of your online accounts, such as **Gmail** or **iCloud**, and import the contacts that you have there. In Windows 11, the **People** app is accessed from the **Mail** app.

 Open the **Mail** app and click on this button in the bottom left-hand corner

2 The current contacts are displayed. Double-click on a contact to view their details

3 Click on a letter at the top of a section to access the alpha search list. Click on a letter to view contacts starting with the selected letter

4 Click on the **Settings** button to add new accounts from which you want to import contacts, such as a Gmail or an iCloud account (in the same way as setting up a new email account). Click on the **Add an account** button to add the required account. The contacts from the linked account are imported to the **People** app

...cont'd

Adding contacts manually

As well as importing contacts, it is also possible to enter them manually into the **People** app.

1 Click on the **New contact** button on the top toolbar

2 Enter details for the new contact, including name, email address and phone number

3 Click on the **Down** arrow next to a field to access additional options for that item

- 📱 Mobile
- 🏠 Home
- 💼 Work
- 📇 Company
- 📟 Pager
- 🖨 Home fax
- 🖨 Work fax

4 Click on the **Save** button at the bottom of the window to create the new contact

Hot tip

Once a contact has been added, select it as in Step 2 on the previous page and click on this button to edit the contact's details.

✏️ Edit

Hot tip

When a contact has been selected, click on the pin icon on the top toolbar and select either **Pin to Taskbar** or **Pin to Start** to pin the contact here. More than three contacts can now be pinned in this way.

📌 Pin to Taskbar

📌 Pin to Start

155

Calendar

The **Calendar** app can be used to record important events and reminders. To view the calendar:

1 Click on the **Calendar** app on the Start menu

 Calendar

2 Click here to view the calendar in **Day**, **Week**, or **Month** mode

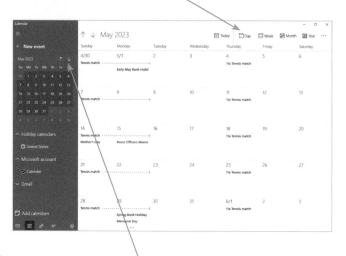

3 Click on these buttons to move between months (or swipe left or right on a touchpad)

Adding events

Events can be added to the calendar and various settings can be applied to them, such as recurrence and reminders.

 Click on a date to create a new event and click on the **New event** button

 Enter an **Event name** and a **Location** at the top of the window

 Click here and select a time for the start and end of the event

| 12:30 PM |
| 1:00 PM |
| 1:30 PM |

 If **All day** is selected, the time fields will not be available

You can scroll **Month** view vertically, a month at a time, up and down, using the arrow buttons.

You can scroll **Week** views horizontally, seven days at a time, using the **Left** and **Right** arrow buttons. Use the scroll bar to move vertically through the hours.

157

Reminders can be set for calendar events, and these appear in the **Notifications area**. Click on this box in Step 2 to set a time period for a reminder.

| Reminder: | 5 minutes |

The **Chat** app is a new feature in Windows 11.

If the **Microsoft Teams** app has already been accessed, some of the initial steps for setting up the **Chat** app may not be required.

For a detailed look at **Microsoft Teams**, see Microsoft Teams in easy steps (visit www.ineasysteps. com).

Chat app

Windows 11 is integrated closely with the collaboration and communication app **Microsoft Teams**. Part of this is the **Chat** app, which is a new feature in Windows 11 and provides text- and video-chat functions, linked to **Microsoft Teams**, but provided through an independent app. To get started with **Chat**:

 Click on the **Chat** icon on the Taskbar

 Click on the **Get started** button

Meet and chat with friends and family

Stay connected with everyone across your life with Microsoft Teams.

Get started

3 Select the Microsoft account to use with the **Chat** app (which links to the parent app, **Microsoft Teams**). The Microsoft account is usually the one you use for signing in with Windows 11

Welcome to Teams

Chat and collaborate in one app.

Pick an account

S

Use another account

 Enter the name you want to appear in the Chat app and click on the **Next** button

Microsoft

Add details

We need a little more info before you can use this app.

First name | Surname
Simon | Watson

Cancel | Next

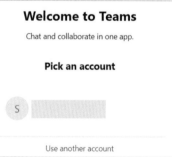

5 Click on the **Let's go** button

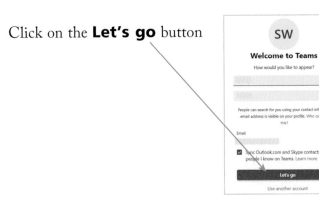

The **Microsoft Teams** app has replaced **Skype** as the default collaboration and communication app within Windows.

6 Click on the **Sync contacts** button to synchronize your contacts from other apps and locations

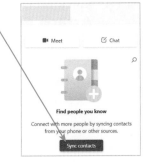

If you prefer to use **Skype**, you can download the app from the Microsoft Store.

7 Click on the options for synchronizing contacts. These will then be available in the **Chat** app

8 Click on the **Chat** app again to access it, ready for text, audio or video chats. Enter a name in the **To:** box to select someone for a conversation

Depending on how you have synchronized your contacts, you may be able to enter the start of someone's name in the **To:** box in Step 8 to select them from your existing contacts, or you may need to enter their full details; i.e. their email address.

...cont'd

The **Format** icon in
Step 8 on page 159 includes options for adding bold, italics, underlining, font color and font size. Format selection can be made before text is added, or to selected text.

9 Click in the text box to enter text for the message

10 Use the icons below the text box to add a range of content to the message; see the next four steps

11 Click on the
Attach Files button
in Step 8 on page
159 and click on the
Upload from my computer option to select
files from your own computer

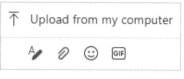

12 Click on the **Emoji** button in Step 8 on page 159 and click on an emoji to add it to the text message

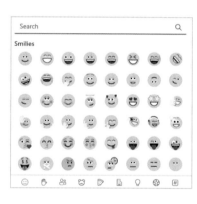

13 Scroll down the emoji page, or click on the toolbar at the bottom of the panel, to access the different categories of emojis

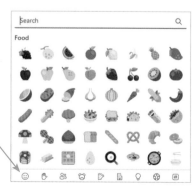

14 Click on the **GIF** button in Step 8 on page 159 and to access animated and graphical GIF images. Click on a GIF to add it to the text message

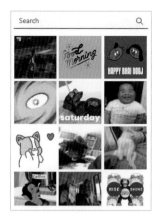

15 A conversation is created within the chat window and continues down the window as more content is added

 16 Click on this button to send a text message

17 Use these buttons in the top right-hand corner of the chat box to, from left to right: start a video call with the person in the conversation; start an audio call with the person in the conversation; and add people for text, video or audio calls

Don't forget

Click on this button in Step 15 and enter the details of a new contact, to add someone to the conversation.

Windows 11 and Office

Windows 11 systems do not normally include **Microsoft Office** as an installed option, unless it gets added as an extra by the system supplier. However, there are several ways you can find facilities to help you work with **Office** documents.

The **Office Online** and **Office Mobile** apps are available at no charge, but have limitations in the functions they are able to provide.

1 Go to **products.office.com/en-us/office-online** to get free use of Office applications via your browser

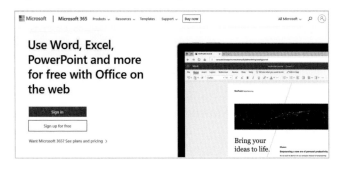

2 If you have a tablet or smartphone, you can search the Microsoft Store to find free mobile versions of **Word**, **PowerPoint**, and **Excel**

Windows 11 includes the **Office** app to help you manage your **Microsoft 365** subscription benefits.

Office

3 For the full versions of the **Office** applications, go to **products. office.com/en-us/try** for a free one-month trial of Microsoft 365, or to take out a subscription to the product

Outlook

With **Microsoft 365** or **Office** (all editions except Home & Student) installed on your Windows 11 system, you'll have **Outlook** as an alternative for email messages and time management.

 Select the entry for **Outlook** in the **All apps** list

The **Microsoft Office** applications may have been pinned to the Start menu, from where you can select the **Outlook** entry.

2 Enter the email address for the account you want to use with Outlook and click on the **Connect** button

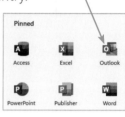

3 Specify a password for the chosen account, then click **Connect** to continue and follow any more options for the selected account

4 Once the account has been added, its details are displayed

Outlook
Account successfully added
IMAP nickvandome@gmail.com
Add another email address
Email address   Next
Advanced options ⌄

...cont'd

5 If you do want to set up **Outlook Mobile** on your phone, check the box before clicking **Done**

The **Done** option can be selected in Step 4 on page 163 to complete the setup, without checking the **Outlook Mobile** option.

☑ Set up Outlook Mobile on my phone, too

Done

6 Enter your phone number and click **Send link** to enable you to complete the setup on the phone

Outlook

Complete your Outlook setup and get the same, great experience while on the go.

Enter your phone number and we'll send a download link

📞 ▪ +1 ▾ 201-555-5555   Send link

Or scan the QR code below

7 Outlook opens on the desktop with Mail selected and with the most recent message displayed

Click the **<** arrow to collapse the **Folder** pane (or the **>** arrow to expand it). Click **More Options (...)** on **Navigation Options...** for **Notes**, **Folders** and **Shortcuts**.

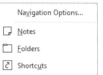

Navigation Options...

☐ Notes
☐ Folders
↺ Shortcuts

8 There are buttons on the **View** switcher to select **Mail**, **Calendar**, **People** and **Tasks**, alongside the **More Options (...)** button for more links

9 Internet

Windows 11 uses the Microsoft Edge internet browser to help you navigate through the web. This chapter shows how to get started with some of its functions and features.

Browsing the web

By default, Windows 11 provides access to the internet via the Microsoft Edge browser.

The **Edge** browser has been updated in Windows 11, with a redesigned interface.

1 Click the **Microsoft Edge** icon on the Taskbar to open the app

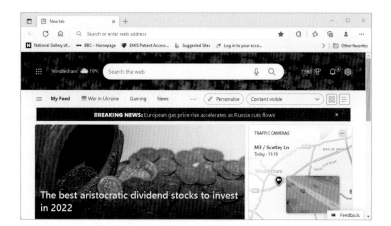

See pages 211-212 for details about connecting to a network for access to the internet.

2 The **Start** screen displays, with a News channel provided by MSN. Scroll down for more items

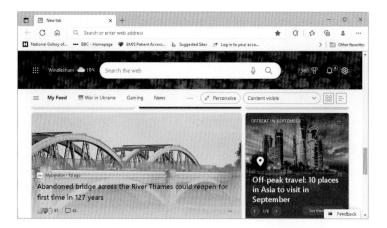

The display image may be much larger than the monitor size, but you can scroll to review the parts that are off-screen.

You can scroll the screen with the mouse wheel, or by clicking the scroll bar that appears when you move the mouse, or by dragging the scroll bar on a touch monitor.

Click in the **Search** box at the top of the Start screen and begin typing your search term – "bbc", for example – to see related Search suggestions

 Choose a Search suggestion – "bbc news", for example – to see a list of web pages matching that term

 Select one of the web pages and explore the commands that are available

Back Forward Refresh Home New tab Address bar

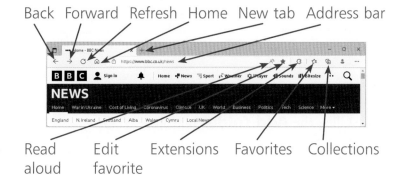

Read aloud   Edit favorite   Extensions   Favorites   Collections

Favorites gives access to the **Favorites bar** and to **Other favorites**, including the reading list and previously visited websites.

Settings and more (**...**) gives access to a variety of options.

Favorites

You can make your more frequently accessed web pages easier to find using **Favorites** in Microsoft Edge. To show the favorites that are currently defined:

You can also display the list of favorites in Microsoft Edge by pressing the **Ctrl** + **Shift** + **O** key combination.

1 Click the **Star** icon on the Microsoft Edge Toolbar, and the favorites will be displayed

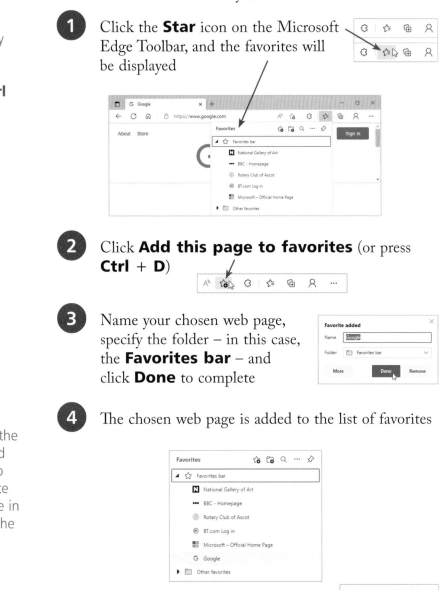

2 Click **Add this page to favorites** (or press **Ctrl** + **D**)

3 Name your chosen web page, specify the folder – in this case, the **Favorites bar** – and click **Done** to complete

4 The chosen web page is added to the list of favorites

You can right-click the **Favorites bar** and select **Open all**, to have all your favorite web pages available in Microsoft Edge at the same time.

5 Click the **Add folder** button to create a new folder on the **Favorites bar**, and specify a folder name – for example, MyProject

...cont'd

By default, Microsoft Edge will show the **Favorites bar** only on a new tab, but you can display it in other situations.

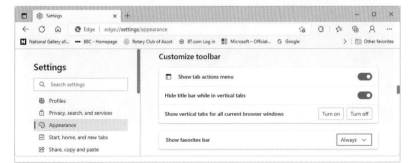

Hot tip

This shows the **Favorites bar**, which is a folder within **Favorites** (note the spellings are localized).

1 Select **Settings and more (…) > Settings**

2 Select **Appearance** and scroll to **Customize toolbar**

Hot tip

You can also show and hide a sidebar that gives access to other apps, by clicking the **Settings and more (…)** button and choosing **Show sidebar** or **Hide sidebar**.

3 Click the **Down** arrow and choose the option to show the **Favorites bar Always**

4 Microsoft Edge will now feature the **Favorites bar**, which appears just below the **Address bar**

169

Immersive Reader

Immersive Reader transforms a web page into a simple format that has fewer distractions – no sidebars, ads, comments, etc.

1 Below is an example of a web page that has **Reading View** enabled

Hot tip

The **Reading View** icon is gray when it is available, and blue when active.

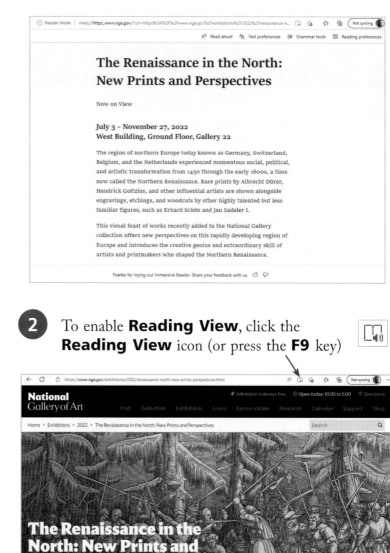

Hot tip

Click on this icon in the **Address bar**, if available, to enable the Edge browser to read the content on the current page being viewed.

2 To enable **Reading View**, click the **Reading View** icon (or press the **F9** key)

Settings

There is an extensive range of settings that can be used with the Edge browser.

 1 Select **Settings and more (...)** and click on the **Settings** button

    ⚙ Settings

 2 The main settings categories are listed in the left-hand sidebar. Click on a category to view its content in the main window

 3 Select the **Appearance** category to apply options for how Edge windows look

 4 Select the **Privacy, search, and services** category to apply a range of security settings

 5 Select the **Start, home, and new tabs** category to apply settings for how certain items open up in the Edge browser

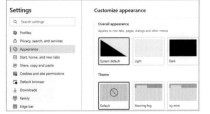

Don't forget

You can clear browsing data that may build up on your system, by selecting **Choose what to clear** in the **Privacy, search, and services** category.

Light and Dark themes

Microsoft Edge offers a choice of two display themes.

 Open a web page and the default **Light** theme will be applied to all displayed Microsoft Edge menus; for example, History

 From **Settings and more (...)** > **Settings**, select **Appearance** in the left-hand sidebar

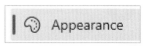

 The Edge themes are displayed

 The selected theme is immediately applied to all displayed menus

 The content of the web page itself is unchanged

Web capture

With Microsoft Edge, you can save web pages, useful when you wish to share information with others.

 1 Open a web page that you want to save and click **Settings and more (…) > Settings**

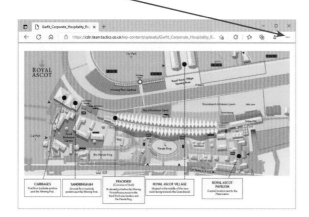

- Performance
- Alerts and tips
- Print   Ctrl+P
- Web capture   Ctrl+Shift+S
- Web select   Ctrl+Shift+X
- Share
- Find on page   Ctrl+F
- Read aloud   Ctrl+Shift+U

2 Click the **Web capture** option and choose an option – **Capture area** or **Capture full page**

3 Here's an example of what **Capture area** looks like:

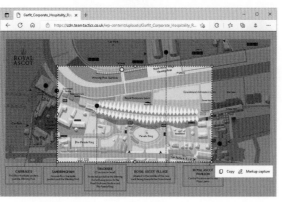

Right-click menus

Additional functionality can be viewed on web pages with the Microsoft Edge browser, by using the right-click option on the mouse. To do this:

You can view multiple pages in Microsoft Edge, each on a separate tab (see the next page).

1 Open a web page in Microsoft Edge

174

2 Right-click an empty part of the page (the mouse pointer remains as an arrow) to get a basic context menu

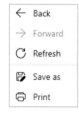

3 Right-click an image with a hyperlink (the mouse pointer becomes a hand) and an image-related context menu appears

Hyperlinks direct you to other website locations. They can be associated with images, graphics and text.

4 There is a more restricted context menu displayed when you right-click text with a hyperlink (again with a hand pointer)

Tabbed browsing

Being able to open several web pages at the same time in different tabs is a standard feature in most web browsers. To do this with Microsoft Edge:

  1 Click on this button at the top of the Microsoft Edge window

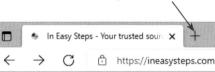

  2 Pages can be opened in new tabs using the smart **Address bar** or from any of the content options that are displayed on the page (which varies by location)

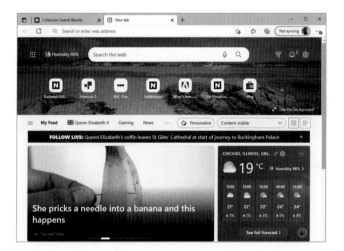

3 All open tabs are displayed at the top of the window. Click and hold on a tab to drag it into a new position

175

Hot tip

The **Start** page for new tabs, as displayed in Step 2, can be changed if required. To do this, open the Microsoft Edge settings and access the **Start, home, and new tabs** section. Check **On** the **Open the new tabs page** heading and select a page in the same way as for selecting a homepage.

Hot tip

Press **Ctrl + T** to add a new tab. Right-click a hyperlink and select **Open in new tab**. A tab with that web page is added.

...cont'd

The options for managing tabs in the Edge browser have been updated in Windows 11.

Once tabs have been opened in the Edge browser, there are a number of options for viewing and managing them.

1 Click on this button at the top of the Microsoft Edge window to view options for managing tabs, including creating a new tab, duplicating the currently active tab, pinning tabs and changing the orientation of open tabs

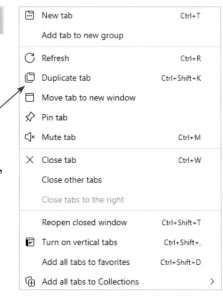

2 Click on this button at the left-hand side of the **Tabs bar** to access more options

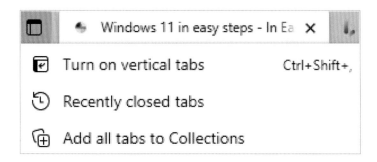

3 Click on the **Turn on vertical tabs** option to change the orientation of the **Tabs bar**

4 The **Tabs bar** is displayed down the left-hand side of the Edge browser window

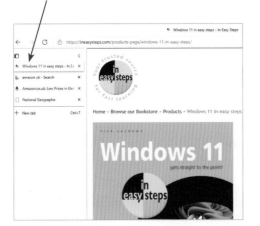

Using vertical tabs is a new feature in Windows 11.

5 Click on this button in Step 4 to minimize the vertical **Tabs bar**

6 Click on this button to expand the minimized **Tabs bar**

Don't forget

The vertical tabs option can be used even if there is only one open tab.

7 Move the cursor over the minimized **Tabs bar** and click on this button to expand it and keep the maximized option in place

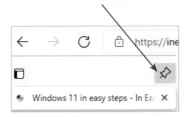

Zooming in on a web page

You may find some web pages difficult to read, especially if you have your monitor set for high resolution. Microsoft Edge also provides a **Zoom** feature. Its methods for zooming the web page include:

Press **F11** on the keyboard to exit full-screen mode.

 Select **Settings and more** (...) and on the **Zoom** entry click the **+** or **-** buttons to zoom in, by 10% initially and then in increments of 25%, or zoom out

 Click on this button to view the Edge window in full-screen mode

 Press **Ctrl +** to zoom in, by 10% initially and then in increments of 25%, or **Ctrl -** to zoom out

 Press **Ctrl 0** to reset to 100%

 If the option with the **Ctrl** key is used, a magnifying glass icon appears in the **Address bar**. Click on the zoom options as required

 Click on the **Reset** button to return to 100% view

10 Windows games

You can access Xbox games in the Microsoft Store, to find a variety of games. With the Xbox app you can also record and share your scores.

Games in Windows 11

There is a limited number of games pre-installed with Windows 11, including **Microsoft Solitaire Collection**. However, you will find many games available in the Microsoft Store, from the **Gaming** tab in the left-hand sidebar. These include many free games, though you should be aware that associated in-game purchases may be suggested during play.

Gaming

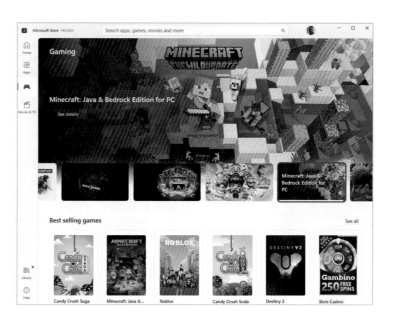

Don't forget

Xbox is Microsoft's video game console, competing with Sony's PlayStation. The Xbox network service allows players to play games online via a broadband connection.

Scroll up the page to see a full selection of available games, or click on the **See all** option next to a games category to view all of the items within it.

Microsoft has integrated Xbox content and gaming services into Windows 11, and provides the **Xbox** app (see page 190). This gives Windows 11 players access to the Xbox network so that they can keep track of their achievements, see what their friends are playing, and be participators in multiplayer games.

Xbox

Xbox console users are also able to stream their Xbox games to their Windows 11 PC or tablet.

Games in the Microsoft Store

To get started with games from the Microsoft Store:

1 Click on the **Microsoft Store** icon on the Taskbar

2 Click on the **Gaming** icon in the left-hand sidebar to access the Gaming homepage within the Microsoft Store

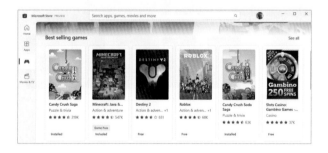

Don't forget

The games that are featured and the games selected for each list will change frequently, but these examples illustrate the types of findings you can expect.

3 Scroll down to see a selection of **Best selling games**. Best sellers include free as well as chargeable games. The Microsoft Store also identifies games you have installed

Hot tip

Click the **Show all** link for any selection, to browse the complete set of games in that group.

4 Scroll on to find a selection of **Top paid games**

...cont'd

5 Scroll on, using the vertical scroll bar or the mouse wheel, and review a selection of **Featured free games** (and click **See all** to explore the complete set)

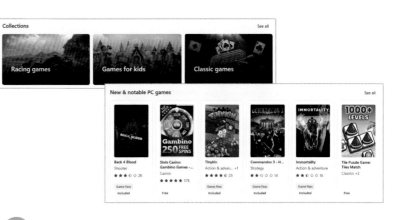

Don't forget

The categories on the Microsoft Store homepage change over time.

6 You can also explore the various **Collections** of games, or view a selection of **New & notable PC games**

Hot tip

Individual games may appear in several groups. For example, games shown in the **Top free** or **Top paid** selections may also be included in the **Trending** or **Collections** selection.

7 Some **See all** categories have a **Filters** button – click in the **All categories** box to view all of the available games categories

Word games

1 Go to the Microsoft Store, and search for games under the term "word search"

2 Select the **Word Search** entry by Steve Nessen, and follow the prompts to install the app on your system

3 Open **Word Search** from the **All apps** list on the **Start** menu

4 Select **Settings** and choose the difficulty level and the type of word list

5 Click the **Back** arrow to exit **Settings**

6 Select **Start**, and play the game. At the **Easy** level, words are vertical or horizontal, and you can see a scrolling list of words you are looking for

7 When you have located all the words, the game ends and your score is displayed

You can choose games that are complex and challenging, such as **Mahjong** and **Solitaire**, or you can choose simple games that are easy and fun to play, such as the **Word Games** collection.

Select **Highscore** to see a list of your results, and select **Trophies** to set yourself some challenges.

Microsoft Solitaire Collection

If you have enjoyed playing **FreeCell** or **Spider Solitaire** in a previous release of Windows, you'll be pleased to find **Microsoft Solitaire Collection** in the Store.

By signing in and creating an Xbox profile (see page 190), you can record the results for all the games you play and share your achievements with other players.

1 Find the game in the Microsoft Store, and note that it is already installed on your system

2 Select the Store entry to see its description. You are advised that there are **In-Game Purchases** options

3 Select **Play** from the Store entry (or select the **Start** menu entry)

4 The app loads up and offers you a choice of **Klondike**, **Spider**, **FreeCell**, **Pyramid** and **TriPeaks**

...cont'd

5 Click on the **Menu** button in the top left-hand corner to access options for playing the game, including the different game versions

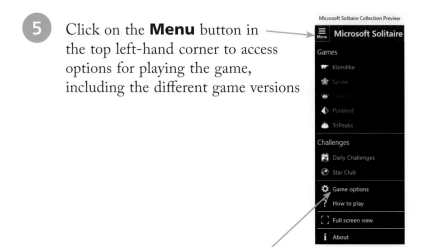

6 Click on the **Game options** item in the previous step to access options for how games operate

7 Select a game as appropriate to start playing it, from either the options in Step 4 or Step 5 on the previous page

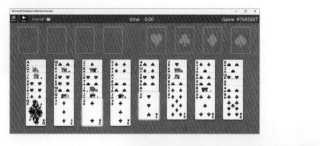

8 If you make a disallowed move, a dialog box will

appear with a related tip. Click **Close** to leave the dialog and return to the game

Microsoft Minesweeper

 Find **Microsoft Minesweeper** in the Microsoft Store to view a description of the game

The process that you follow to install and play **Minesweeper** is typical for Xbox games on Windows 11 PCs.

 Click **Get** and follow the prompts to install the game

 Select the app from the **All apps** list on the Start menu to open the game. An introduction screen is displayed before accessing the app's homepage

4 Choose one of the game types such as **Easy 9x9** to get started, or a more advanced level depending on your experience and ability

5 A tutorial option is displayed. Click **Next** to move through the tutorial, or **Skip** to close it

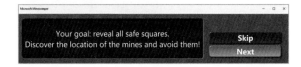

6. A board at the selected level is displayed. The first click is safe, but after that you must check before selecting a cell as safe or potentially mined. Each number indicates the number of mines next to it

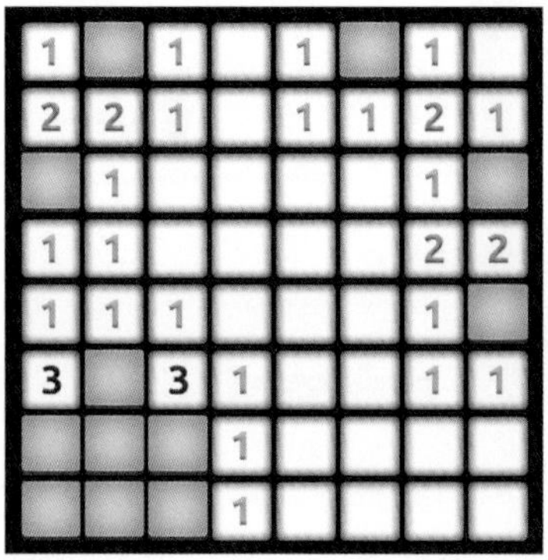

7. If you go wrong and click on a square containing a mine, the results will be explosive and the game will terminate

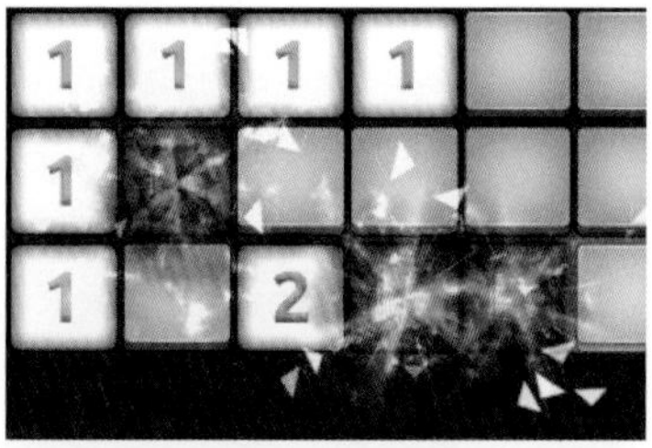

8. Get it right, and you are treated to fireworks at the end of the game and the mines are displayed

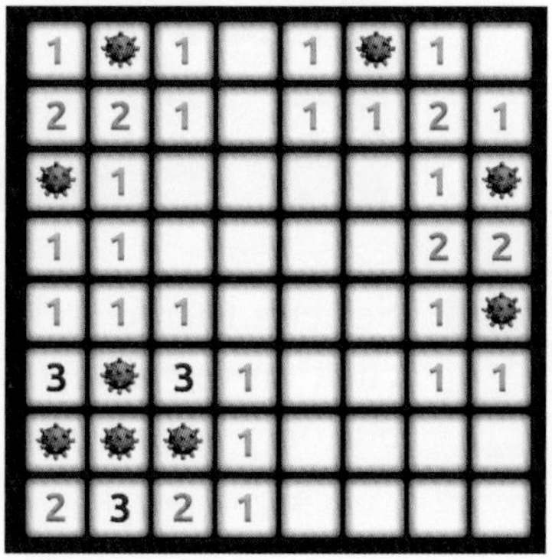

9. Your scores are recorded and can be made available to the Xbox app (and your Xbox gamertag – see page 190) so that they can be shared with other players

Don't forget

You use the numbers displayed to help deduce whether a square is safe to uncover. Right-click a suspect square to add a flag, or left-click a safe cell. On a touchscreen, you would press and hold for a flag, or tap for a safe cell.

Microsoft Mahjong

1 Locate the game in the Microsoft Store, and click the **Get** button to install it, then pin it to the Start menu if required

This game has four skill levels, with about two dozen puzzles for each. It can be played with keyboard, mouse or by touch.

2 Click on the required icon on the **Start** menu (or select it in the **All apps** area)

3 Click on the **Themes** button to select an overall theme for the look of the game

4 Select a theme and click on the **OK** button

5 Click on the **Menu** button
to access options for playing
the game, including the
different game versions and a
How to Play tutorial

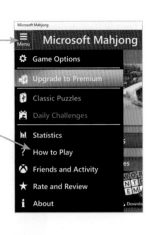

6 Click on the **Menu** button again to exit the menu
and select a puzzle to play. Use the tabs at the top
of the window to select **Easy**, **Medium**, **Hard** or
Expert levels

The first time you
play, you are offered
a tutorial to help
you learn the basic
operations of the
game. You can skip
the tutorial if you
wish.

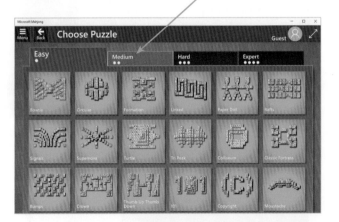

7 Complete the
selected puzzle.
Fireworks are
displayed when
you complete a
puzzle, and the
next puzzle is
available

189

The first time you play a Windows 11 Xbox game, you'll be assigned an account and a gamertag associated with your Microsoft account, to identify you to other players.

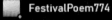
FestivalPoem774

The Xbox app opens with the **Game Pass** option selected. This is a subscription option for access to a wider range of games, some of which can be played with other players, using the Xbox app. Click on the **Community** option in the sidebar in Step 1 to find other Xbox players, with whom you can play online games. The free Xbox games can be played without the need for a **Game Pass**.

Xbox app

The Xbox app provides access to Windows 11 versions of Xbox games. You do not have to own an Xbox games device.

1   Click the **Xbox** icon on the Start menu and Xbox opens with your gamertag

Xbox

2   Click on your gamertag icon to access menu options for the Xbox app

3   Click on the **Settings** option to view the full range of settings for the Xbox app

4   Click on the **My Library** option in the sidebar in Step 1 to view your Xbox games and add new ones

11 Music and pictures

This chapter shows how you can create recordings, play CDs and convert tracks to computer files. You can also manage movie and TV show collections, and create albums and slideshows from digital images and photos.

Cortana is the Windows 11 digital voice assistant that can be used for voice search. To set this up, click on the **Search** icon on the Taskbar and enter "Cortana" as the search criteria. Click on the **Cortana** option when it appears on the search results page, to open Cortana and start making voice searches.

Sound card and speakers

The sound card in your computer processes the information from apps such as **Media Player** or **Cortana** and sends audio signals to your computer's speakers.

To review and adjust your sound setup:

 Click on the **Settings** app on the Taskbar

 Click on the **System** category in the left-hand sidebar

 Click on the **Sound** option

> Sound
> Volume levels, output, input, sound devices

 Select options for sound **Output** as required. Click on the **Speakers** option to view the properties for your computer's speakers

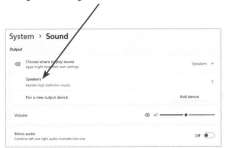

 Select options for the speakers, including allowing apps to use them, general volume settings and volume settings for the left and right channels

Recording

With a sound card in your system, you can make voice recordings from a microphone or other audio sources. To access settings for your microphone:

 Access the **Sound** settings as shown on the previous page

 Select options for sound input as required. Click on the **Microphone** option to view the properties of your computer's microphone

When you've set up your microphone and speakers, you'll be able to use the **Cortana** digital assistant to ask questions and get audio responses.

 Click on the **Test your microphone** option to do a sound test for the microphone

On the main **Sound** page, in the **Advanced** section, click on **Troubleshoot common sound problems** for either **Output devices** or **Input devices**

Click on the **More sound settings** option in Step 4 to access more options for individual devices.

Media Player

The **Media Player** app can be used to play and manage digital music with Windows 11. To use it:

Media Player is the video and audio player for Windows 11, and replaces the **Groove Music** and **Windows Media Player** apps.

Click on the **Menu** button in the sidebar navigation to display the titles for the icons.

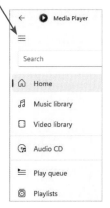

Click **Shuffle and play** to listen to tunes selected randomly from your collection.

1 Select **Media Player** from the Start menu or **All apps** list

2 The **Media Player** homepage is displayed, with the left-hand sidebar used for navigating around

3 You may need to add the **Music** folder from your PC to the **Media Player** app, by clicking the **Add folder** button in the **Music library** section

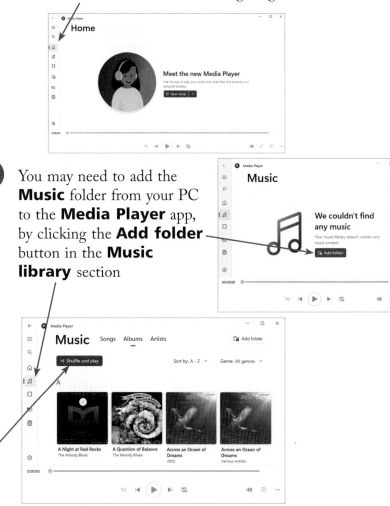

4 Click on **Music library** in the sidebar to choose to list songs, albums (below) or artists. The albums in your Music library will be listed in alphabetical sequence and with cover pictures displayed

...cont'd

Details of the current track are shown, and the progression is illustrated by a slider at the bottom of the window.

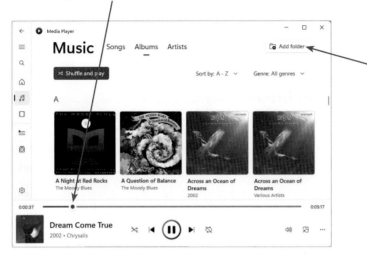

You can click the **Add folder** button to specify another folder that contains music.

For more details about using the **Music library**, see page 199.

5 To change the sequence in which albums are displayed, you should click **Sort by** and then choose an option: **A - Z**, **Release year**, **Artist** or **Date added**

You can play albums that are on your OneDrive on any device where you sign in with your Microsoft account.

6 To filter the list by type of album, click **Genre** and choose from the extensive list of genres offered

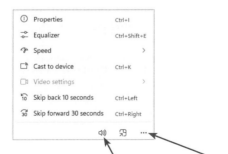

The **Mini player** in Step 7 is a pop-out window that contains the music controls for the **Media Player** so that it can be used when other apps are accessed.

7 You can adjust the volume, switch to the **Mini player**, or select **More options (...)** to display a list of actions that are available

Playing audio CDs

Although playing an audio CD on a computer may seem a little old-fashioned in a world of streaming music, it still plays an important role as there are still many CDs that are used for music. To do this:

 Insert an audio CD into your computer's CD drive and open the **Media Player** app

 Click on this button (**Audio CD**) in the left-hand sidebar

 Details of the audio CD are displayed in the main window

Hot tip

If you want to copy tracks from an audio CD onto your computer, this can be done with a process called ripping (see page 198 for details).

Vivaldi: The Four Seasons, Etc.

Riccardo Chailly: Bologna Teatro Communale Philharmonic Orchestra

1995 • Classical Period • 19 tracks • 01:10:17 run time

▷ Play   ⤫ Shuffle and play   + Add to   🎵 Rip CD   ⚙ Rip settings   ...

1. Vivaldi: Violin Concerto In F, RV 286, "Per La Solennità...	Riccardo Chailly: Bologna Teatro Com...	1995	Classical Period	05:32
2. Vivaldi: Violin Concerto In F, RV 286, "Per La Solennità...	Riccardo Chailly: Bologna Teatro Com...	1995	Classical Period	03:04
3. Vivaldi: Violin Concerto In F, RV 286, "Per La Solennità...	Riccardo Chailly: Bologna Teatro Com...	1995	Classical Period	04:03
4. Vivaldi: Concerto Funebre	Riccardo Chailly: Bologna Teatro Com...	1995	Classical Period	08:50
5. Vivaldi: Concerto In G Minor "Per L'Orchestra Di Dresd...	Riccardo Chailly: Bologna Teatro Com...	1995	Classical Period	03:43

 Click on a track to select it and click on the **Play** button

 Click on the **Shuffle and play** button to play the tracks of the CD in a random order

6. Click on a track to select it and click on the **Play** button

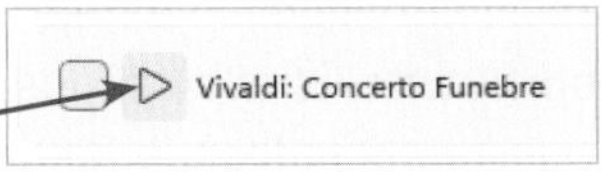
Vivaldi: Concerto Funebre

7. As a track plays, the music controls are available at the bottom of the window

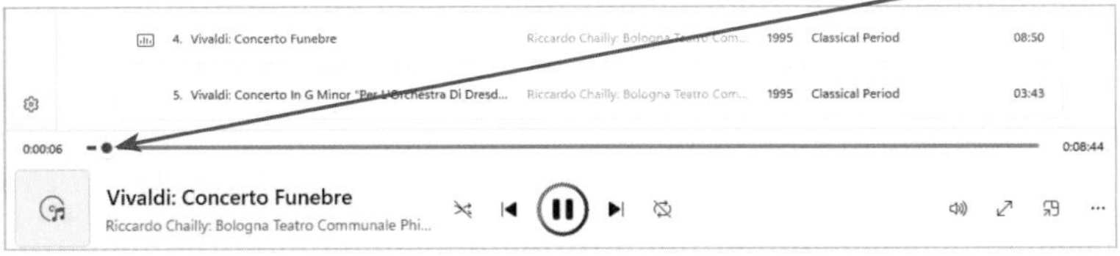
4. Vivaldi: Concerto Funebre
Riccardo Chailly: Bologna Teatro Com...
1995
Classical Period
08:50
5. Vivaldi: Concerto In G Minor "Per L'Orchestra Di Dresd...
Riccardo Chailly: Bologna Teatro Com...
1995
Classical Period
03:43
0:00:06
0:08:44
Vivaldi: Concerto Funebre
Riccardo Chailly: Bologna Teatro Communale Phi...

8. Use these controls to, from left to right: shuffle the tracks on the CD; go to the start of the current track being played; pause or play the current track; go to the end of the current track; and repeat the current track being played

9. Use these controls to, from left to right: change the volume; display the Media Player in full screen; minimize the Media Player window so that it only takes up a small part of the screen; and access the **More options** panel

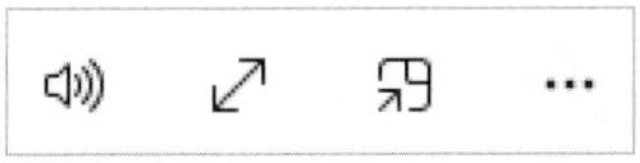

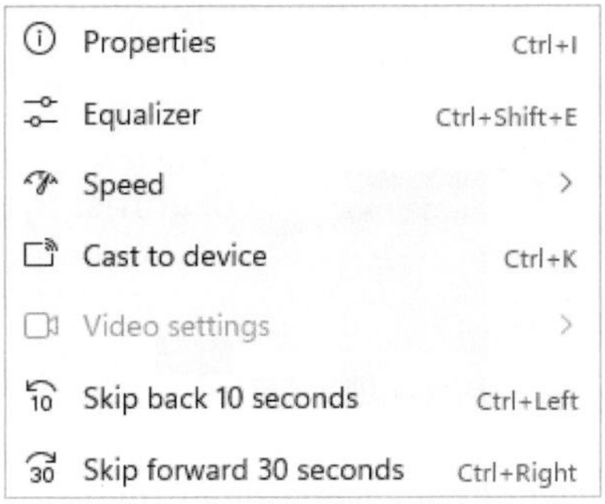
Properties Ctrl+I
Equalizer Ctrl+Shift+E
Speed
Cast to device Ctrl+K
Video settings
Skip back 10 seconds Ctrl+Left
Skip forward 30 seconds Ctrl+Right

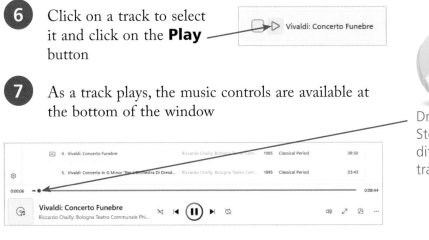

Hot tip

Drag the slider in Step 7 to move to different points in a track.

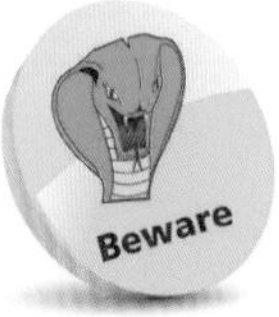
Beware

Be careful not to set the volume too high for an audio CD, particularly for an extended period of time.

Copying tracks

In addition to playing an audio CD with a Windows 11 computer, it is also possible to copy the tracks onto your computer, which is known as ripping. To do this:

1 Insert an audio CD into your computer's CD drive and open the **Media Player** app. Click on the **Audio CD** button, as shown on page 196

2 Click on the **Rip settings** button

Click on the **Edit info** button in Step 2 to view information about the current audio CD. Click on the **Update album info online** option to view any available updated details about the item.

3 Apply settings for copying the CD, as required, and click on the **Save** button

> **Rip settings**
>
> **Format**
> We'll save music to your device using this format. AAC is a good choice if you're unsure.
>
> AAC ∨
>
> **Bit rate**
> Higher bitrates provide higher quality audio, but the files will take up more storage space.
>
> 256 kbps (recommended for music) ∨
>
> Save   Cancel

4 Click on the **Rip CD** button to copy the audio tracks to the Media Player app. The progress is shown next to each track

Once an audio CD has been ripped, it is available in the **Music library** section of the Media Player app.

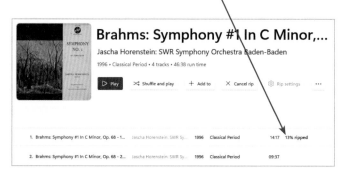

Brahms: Symphony #1 In C Minor,...
Jascha Horenstein: SWR Symphony Orchestra Baden-Baden
1996 • Classical Period • 4 tracks • 46:38 run time

▷ Play   ⤭ Shuffle and play   + Add to   ✕ Cancel rip   ⚙ Rip settings   ...

1. Brahms: Symphony #1 In C Minor, Op. 68 - 1...   Jascha Horenstein: SWR Sy...   1996   Classical Period   14:17   13% ripped

2. Brahms: Symphony #1 In C Minor, Op. 68 - 2...   Jascha Horenstein: SWR Sy...   1996   Classical Period   09:37

Music library

The **Music library** in the **Media Player** app is the section where content that has been copied to the app can be viewed and accessed.

 1 Click on this button (**Music library**) in the left-hand sidebar

 2 Items in the **Music library** are displayed in the main window. In this case, the audio CD copied on the previous page is displayed in the **Music library**

The most recently added item appears at the top of the **Music library** window.

3 Scroll down the window to view more items in the **Music library**

4 Use the buttons at the top of the **Music library** to view content according to **Songs**, **Albums** and **Artists**

5 Use these buttons in either **Songs** or **Albums** view to sort items alphabetically or by genre

Sort by: A - Z ∨   Genre: All genres ∨

Playlists

You can create playlists containing selected songs from several albums, perhaps related to a particular theme or style.

 Open the **Media Player** app and select **Music library** > **Albums**

 Click an album to list the songs it contains, and select individual songs for your list

Hot tip

Create as many playlists as you need, to help organize the music files on your system.

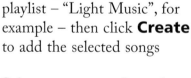

 Click the **See more** button and select **Add to** > **New playlist**

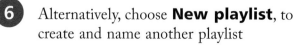 You are prompted to name your playlist – "Light Music", for example – then click **Create** to add the selected songs

Select more songs from the same or a different album, and add to your existing playlist

Alternatively, choose **New playlist**, to create and name another playlist

7 To check the playlists that you have on your system, click **Playlist** on the Icon bar (or press **Ctrl** + **Y**)

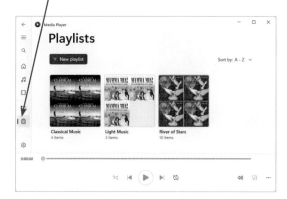

In this example, three separate playlists have been created in **Media Player**.

8 Select a playlist and click the **Play** button

If you right-click the **Mini player** and select **Properties** (or press **Ctrl** + **I**) you will see the details of the current track – Title, Album, Track, Genre, Bit rate, File location, etc.

9 With **Play** selected, the icons on the lower left of the Media Player panel are activated, and you can click the **Mini player** button (or press **Ctrl** + **M**)

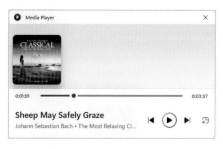

201

Movies & TV

1 Select the **Movies & TV** icon from the **Start** menu to start the app

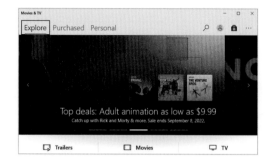

Hot tip

You can also add movie and TV content to your Windows 11 computer or mobile device by downloading from **YouTube**, or purchasing or renting from the Microsoft Store.

2 The app opens with **Explore** selected, showing featured movies. Select **Trailers** for more movies

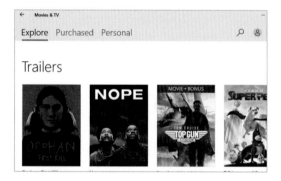

Don't forget

The **Movies & TV** app may be called **Films & TV** in some regions. The items displayed will differ over time.

3 Click on the **Personal** tab to see the item that you have saved to the **Movies & TV** app

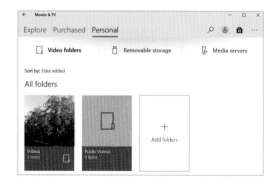

Hot tip

Click the links to see specified selections, or simply scroll the **Explore** page to see subsets of each.

4 Click **More options (…)** > **Settings** to select the download quality (HD or SD)

5 Select **Choose where we look for videos**, to specify libraries or folders to search

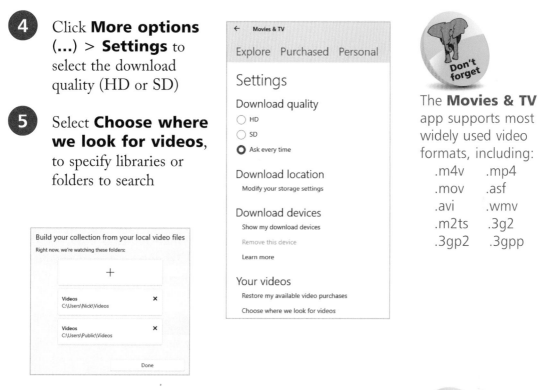

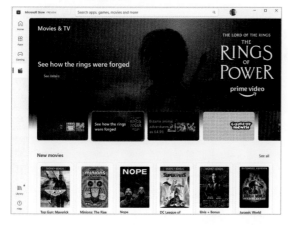

The **Movies & TV** app supports most widely used video formats, including:

.m4v	.mp4
.mov	.asf
.avi	.wmv
.m2ts	.3g2
.3gp2	.3gpp

6 Click the **Microsoft Store** icon to open the Store with **Movies & TV** selected

Scroll down to see selections of **New**, **Top selling** and **Featured** movies and TV shows, and you can also search for movies by genre.

7 Review the content, and purchase and install any items that you desire

Digital pictures

There are a number of ways you can obtain digital pictures:

- Internet (e.g. saving images from art or photography websites).
- Scanner (copies of documents, photographs or slides).
- Digital camera (photographs and movies).
- Email attachments and faxes.

Website pictures will usually be stored as JPEG (.jpg) files, which are compressed to minimize the file size. This preserves the full color range but there is some loss of quality. Some images such as graphic symbols and buttons will use the GIF (.gif) format, which restricts color to 256 shades to minimize the file size. To copy a digital image from a website such as **images.nga.gov**:

You can right-click and save a picture even when only part of it is visible on the screen.

 Right-click the image, then select the **Save image as** option

 Accept the suggested file name, or provide an amended version if desired, then click **Save**

3 To view the saved images, right-click **Start** and select **File Explorer** > **Pictures**, then select the appropriate sub-folder

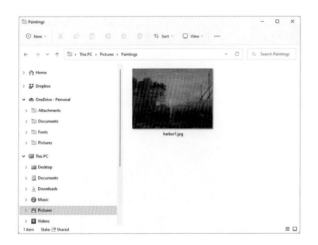

4 To explore the folder more easily, select the **View** button, then choose **Extra large icons**

Beware

Windows Photo Viewer is offered on systems that have been upgraded to Windows 11 from a previous version of Windows. It is not made available on fresh installs of Windows 11.

5 Double-click an image to see it in the default picture viewer

6 Right-click the image, select **Open with**, then choose another app to see the default viewer and other options

Photos app

Photos can be viewed and managed with the pre-installed **Photos** app. To use this:

1 Click on the **Photos** app from the Start menu or the Taskbar

2 The **Photos** app opens at the **Collection** section, displaying the latest items that have been added

3 Click on a photo to view it, with the related toolbar at the top of the window

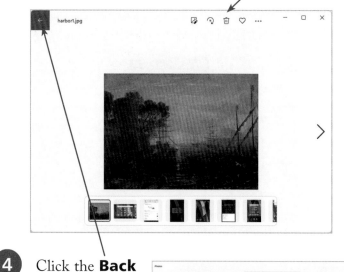

4 Click the **Back** button to go back to the **Collection** page and view all of the app's contents

You can click the **Folders** option to choose source folders from your local system or your OneDrive.

5 Click on the **Albums** tab to see any albums that have been created, or to create a **New album**

The **Photos** app will automatically organize your photographs (by date) into albums of related photos, choosing those it identifies as the best, although you can edit the selection.

6 Click **See more (...)** > **Settings** and scroll through the list of facilities for managing the **Photos** app

7 In **Settings**, click **Add a folder** to specify where the **Photos** app finds content, and click the **On/Off** button for showing cloud-only content from OneDrive

207

Editing photos

You can use the **Photos** app to edit pictures. Open a picture from your collection, and the toolbar across the top offers options to handle or adjust the image.

In addition to **Edit image**, the **Photos** tools include **Rotate, Delete, Add to favorites**, and **See more (...)**.

1 Click the **Edit image** icon (or press **Ctrl + E**) and explore the options offered

Click on the **Adjustment** option on the top toolbar to access options for editing the color elements of a photo, including brightness, contrast and exposure.

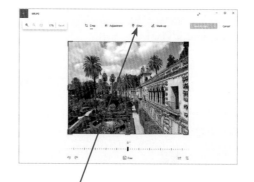

If you edit an image, you can click **Save as copy**, creating a new image with the changes applied.

2 Click the **Filter** option to view the wide range that is available, or choose the **Auto-Enhance** option

12 Networking

This chapter shows how to create a network for access to the internet and also to share content with other devices that are connected to the network.

Creating a network

You have a network when you have several devices that exchange information over a wire or over radio waves (wireless). The simplest network consists of one computer and a router that links to the internet. You can add a second computer, to share internet access and exchange information with the other computer. When the PCs are Windows 11-based, a network can help share data.

To make connections like these, your system will require components of the following types:

- Ethernet twisted-pair cables, for the wired portion.

- A router to manage the network connections.

- An internet modem, which may be integrated with the router.

- An adapter for each computer (wired or wireless).

Setting up the components

The steps you will need, and the most appropriate sequence to follow, will depend on the specific options on your system. However, the main steps will include:

- Install network adapters in the computers, where necessary (in most cases, these will be pre-installed in the computer).

- Set up or verify the internet connection – this should be provided by your Internet Service Provider (ISP).

- Configure the wireless router or access point. (This could involve installing software for the router, which may be provided on a CD or DVD. Some routers will be automatically recognized by Windows 11.)

- Start up Windows on your PC.

Windows 11 is designed to automate as much of the network setup task as possible.

Hot tip

You may already have some, or all, of these elements in operation if you have an existing network running a previous version of Windows.

Connecting to a network

You can connect your computers to form a network using Ethernet cables and adapters, or by setting up your wireless adapters and routers. When you start up each computer, Windows 11 will examine the current configuration and discover any new networks that have been established since the last start-up. You can check this, or connect manually to a network, from within the **Wi-Fi** settings from the **Network & internet** section of **Settings**. To do this:

1 Open the **Settings** app and click on the **Network & internet** tab

> | ▼   Network & internet

2 With no network currently connected, drag the **Wi-Fi** button **On**

> **Network & internet**
>
> 🌐   **Not connected**
> You aren't connected to any networks   Troubleshoot
>
> 📶   **Wi-Fi**
> Connect, manage known networks, metered network   On 🔘 ›
>
> 🖥   **Ethernet**
> Authentication, IP and DNS settings, metered network   ›

3 Click on the **Show available networks** option

> 📡   Show available networks

> **Network & internet › Wi-Fi**
>
> 📶   Wi-Fi   On 🔘
>
> 📡   Show available networks   ⌄

4 Click on the required network

> 📶   PLUSNET-TXJ5
>
> 📶   PLUSNET-TXJ5-5g
>   Secured
>
>   ☑ Connect automatically
>
>   Connect
>
> 📶   Virgin Media

5 Click on the **Connect** button

Beware

The most common type of network for connecting to is the internet.

Beware

If your network is unavailable for any reason, this will be noted in Step 2.

...cont'd

6 Enter a password for the router to be used to connect to the Wi-Fi network

> PLUSNET-TXJ5-5g
> Secured
> Enter the network security key
>
> ●●●●●●●●●
>
> You can also connect by pushing the button on the router.
>
> Next   Cancel

7 Click on the **Next** button

8 If the connection is successful, the network name is shown as **Connected**

> PLUSNET-TXJ5-5g
> Connected, secured

9 Connected networks are shown at the top of the **Network & internet** settings window

> Nick Vandome
> nickvandome@gmail.com
>
> **Network & internet**
>
> Find a setting
>
> Wi-Fi (PLUSNET-TXJ5)
> Connected, secured
>
> System
> Bluetooth & devices
> Network & internet
> Personalization
>
> Properties
> Private network
> 2.4 GHz
>
> Data usage
> 12.38 GB, last 30 days
>
> Wi-Fi
> Connect, manage known networks, metered network
> On

10 Click on the **Data usage** button to see which apps are using the most data on the network

> ··· > Advanced network settings > **Data usage**
>
> 12 MB
> From the last 30 days
>
> Enter data limit
> Windows can help you track data usage to stay under your limit—we'll warn you when you're close, but it won't change your data plan
>
> Wi-Fi (PLUSNET-TXJ ⌄
> Enter limit
>
> Usage statistics
>
> msedge.exe   3 MB
> firefox.exe   2 MB
> Dropbox.exe   1 MB
> System   1 MB

Beware

If you are using a public hotspot Wi-Fi connection, such as in a café or an airport, this may not be as secure as your home network.

Connecting from the Taskbar

It is also possible to connect to a network from the Taskbar.

1 Move the mouse cursor over the **Network** icon on the right of the Taskbar

2 This shows **No internet access**, **Connections available**

No internet access
Connections available

ENG
US

3 Click on the icon to display the connections and select your main wireless network

Available

← Wi-Fi

PLUSNET-TXJ5-5g

4 Check the **Connect automatically** box and then click **Connect**

← Wi-Fi

PLUSNET-TXJ5-5g
Secured

☑ Connect automatically

Connect

5 Connect to the network in the same way as shown on pages 211-212

shown on pages 211-212

Don't forget

Cabled PCs usually get added automatically. When you bring a new wireless PC into the network, you'll need to set up the connection.

Beware

Your system may detect other wireless networks that are in the vicinity, so make sure to select the correct entry.

213

Don't forget

Your computer will now always connect to that network when it comes into range. You can have numerous wireless connections defined; for example, home, office and an internet café.

Network & internet settings

To access the settings for creating networks and gaining access to the internet:

 Click on the **Settings** app on the Taskbar and select **Network & internet**

 All of the relevant network and internet options are displayed

Network & internet

Wi-Fi (PLUSNET-TXJ5-5g) ⓘ Connected, secured	Properties Public network 5 GHz	Data usage 21.83 GB, last 30 days >

Wi-Fi
Connect, manage known networks, metered network — On ⬤ >

Ethernet
Authentication, IP and DNS settings, metered network — >

VPN
Add, connect, manage — >

Mobile hotspot
Share your internet connection — Off ⬤ >

Airplane mode
Stop wireless communication — Off ⬤ >

Proxy
Proxy server for Wi-Fi and Ethernet connections — >

Dial-up
Set up a dial-up internet connection — >

Advanced network settings
View all network adapters, network reset — >

Hot tip

When you select the **Network & internet** option, you can enable **Airplane mode** to disable wireless communication if you are on a flight where this is required.

 Select options as required. For instance, to create a wireless network, click on the **Wi-Fi** option

Network & internet › Wi-Fi

Wi-Fi — On ⬤

Show available networks — ∨

Manage known networks
Add, remove, and edit networks — >

Hardware properties
View and manage Wi-Fi adapter properties — >

Get help
Give feedback

 To create a network with a cable, click on the **Ethernet** option

Network & internet › Ethernet

Ethernet
Not connected — ∧

Authentication settings — Edit

Metered connection
Some apps might work differently to reduce data usage when you're connected to this network — Off ⬤

Set a data limit to help control data usage on this network

IP assignment: — Automatic (DHCP) — Edit

DNS server assignment: — Automatic (DHCP) — Edit

Manufacturer: — Broadcom Corporation — Copy
Description: — Broadcom NetLink (TM) Gigabit Ethernet
Driver version: — 15.6.1.3
Physical address (MAC): — 20-89-84-6A-FB-58

Get help
Give feedback

Sharing options

If you have printers, folders or files you want to share with other users and devices on your network:

 Select **Settings** > **Network & internet**

 Click on **Advanced network settings**

	Advanced network settings
	View all network adapters, network reset

 Click on the **Advanced sharing settings** option

More settings

Advanced sharing settings
Change network discovery and sharing settings

 Drag the **File and printer sharing** button **On**, for either **Private** or **Public** networks

Private networks	∧
Network discovery Your PC can find and be found by other devices on the network	On ⬤
☑ Set up network connected devices automatically	
File and printer sharing Allow others on the network to access shared files and printers on this device	On ⬤
Public networks	Current profile ∧
Network discovery Your PC can find and be found by other devices on the network	On ⬤
File and printer sharing Allow others on the network to access shared files and printers on this device	On ⬤

If no one else is going to be accessing your computer or printer, and you don't want to access anyone else's, then you won't have to worry about the sharing options.

If you are sharing over a network, you should be able to access the **Public** folder on another computer (providing that **Network discovery** is turned **On**). If you are the administrator of the other computer, you will also be able to access your own **Home** folder, although you will need to enter the required password for this.

...cont'd

Sharing folders and files

You can share content from your Windows 11 computer with other people.

To share folders:

 In **File Explorer**, right-click on the folder and click on **Show more options** from the menu

 Show more options

 Select **Give access to** > **Specific people...**

Give access to > Remove access
                    Specific people...

 Enter the details of the person with whom you want to share the folder

← Network access

Choose people to share with

Type a name and then click Add, or click the arrow to find someone.

	Add
Name	Permission Level
Nick Vandome (nickvandome@gmail.com)	Owner

I'm having trouble sharing

Share   Cancel

To share a file:

 In **File Explorer**, select a file to be shared and click on this button on the File Explorer **Menu bar**

Select a person with whom you want to share the file, and the method of sharing – e.g. **Mail**

Share 1 item

Share to

EV   LV   Y   LV
Eilidh   Lucy Vandome YourFamily_952 Lucy Vandome
Vandome   37f69401b49c...

Nearby sharing   Everyone

No devices found nearby
Make sure other devices have nearby sharing turned on

Share with   All apps >

Mail   Dropbox for S   Fresh Paint   Microsoft
         mode   Teams

Nearby sharing

Windows 11 can also send items such as files, links and photos to nearby PCs over Bluetooth (assuming your PC has this connectivity). To do this:

1   Select **Settings** > **System** > **Nearby sharing**

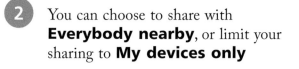

2   You can choose to share with **Everybody nearby**, or limit your sharing to **My devices only**

3   Open **File Explorer**, select a file you wish to share and click the **Share** button

4   Any devices with **Nearby sharing** enabled are detected, and you can choose the one you want

5   Check the status of **Nearby sharing** in **Quick Settings** (see page 67). Click the associated button to switch between **On** and **Off**

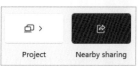

Hot tip

Nearby sharing is similar to Apple's **AirDrop**. However, it will initially only work between two Windows 11 PCs that have the feature enabled. You can't yet share from mobile or other operating systems.

Beware

If **Nearby sharing** is not already enabled when you select a file to share, click on the **Sharing off** button and activate it accordingly.

217

Mobile hotspot

You can use the internet connection on your Windows 11 PC to allow devices to access the internet when the router is not accessible, or when you don't want to reveal your main network password, using **Mobile hotspot**.

 Open **Settings** from the Taskbar, select **Network & internet**, then click the **Mobile hotspot** option

((ᵠ))	Mobile hotspot
	Share your internet connection

Network & internet › Mobile hotspot

Mobile hotspot	On ⬤
Share my internet connection from	Wi-Fi ⌄
Share over	Wi-Fi ⌄
Power saving When no devices are connected, automatically turn off mobile hotspot	On ⬤
Properties	^

Network properties	Edit
Name:	NICKLAPTOP 0635
Password:	e78O4(79
Devices connected:	0 of 8

 Click the **Off/On** button to turn on **Mobile hotspot**, and note the network name and password

 If your PC has both Ethernet and Wi-Fi, you can use either to support the mobile hotspot

3 Note that if your PC has Ethernet only, and no Wi-Fi, it will be unable to offer the **Mobile hotspot** facility

13 Security and maintenance

This chapter details how to get help and support for Windows 11 and also some of the security features that can be used to stay safe and secure.

Windows 11 features a comprehensive set of help facilities including apps, wizards and online support services. Users new to Windows 11 should explore the **Tips** app.

You can select the **All apps** entry and choose **Pin to Start**, and then access **Tips** from the **Pinned** section of the **Start** menu.

The **Get Started** app provides a similar function to the **Tips** app.

Tips app

Included with Windows 11 is the **Tips** app to help you learn about the operating system, with detailed instructions, slideshows and videos covering a range of features and functions of Windows 11.

 Select **Tips** from **All apps**, and the app opens with a number of sections

You are offered sets of tips in slide format, helping you get around in Windows 11, discussing how to take advantage of widgets and reviewing a number of keyboard shortcuts.

Select **See what's new** for a slide presentation highlighting the latest features in Windows 11 and acting as a lead-in to the topics and tips provided in the **Tips** app.

More topics

Scroll down to find more recommended topics, helping you to personalize your PC and to stay safer while using it. There's also an option to show all available tips.

Please note that the numbers and the specific tips that are offered may change over time.

Show all tips

This is the full set of tips, with 18 topics and a total of 136 tips, including File management (7 tips), Gaming (5 tips), Touch keyboard (10 tips) and Use your pen (5 tips).

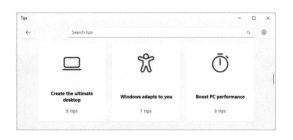

Note that you can flag a tip to indicate the following:

This is helpful

Select a topic – for example, **Tips for Microsoft Edge** – to review the tips that it offers.

This is not helpful

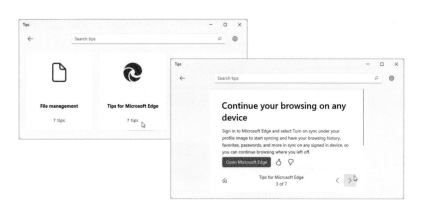

Don't forget

Windows 11 doesn't provide the local help information found in earlier versions, but the **Microsoft Support** website has extensive help on all Microsoft products.

Hot tip

The products listed are based on your setup and on the PCs and devices associated with your Microsoft account. Click **More Microsoft Products** in Step 1 to list others.

Microsoft Support

If the **Tips** app does not answer your questions, you can review the information offered by **Microsoft Support**.

 Open **support.microsoft.com** and sign in to your Microsoft account

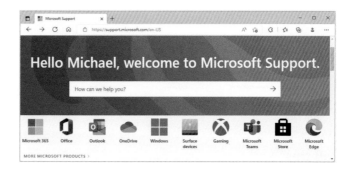

 Select a product – for example, **Windows** – to see the help information that is available

3 Scroll down to select your version and choose one of the related topics

4 Scroll down to reveal **Trending topics**

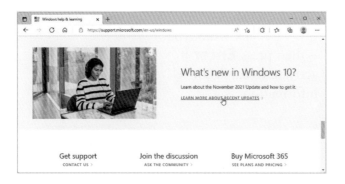

5 Continue scrolling to learn about recent updates

Hot tip

The topics presented will be the most currently sought after, so you can expect the list to change from time to time.

6 Select **Ask the Community** to post questions, follow discussions or share your knowledge with other users

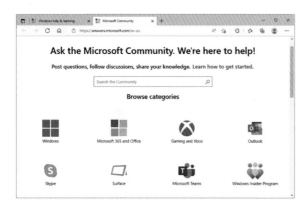

Hot tip

You must be connected to the internet to use the **Get Help** app, and it is recommended that you are signed in with your Microsoft account.

Don't forget

A plain language outline of your problem is best, since it will be matched against queries that other users have submitted.

Get Help app

If you fail to find the answers you need with the usual help facilities, you can try using the **Get Help** app.

1 Select the **Get Help** entry from the **All apps** list

2 **Get Help** asks for details of your problem so that it can find appropriate help and support

3 Enter your query – in this case, just a file type – then press **Enter** to activate a search for related information

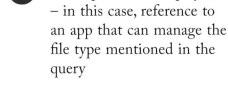

4 The top result is displayed – in this case, reference to an app that can manage the file type mentioned in the query

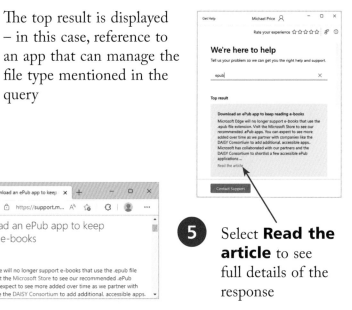

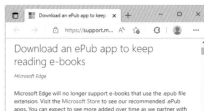

5 Select **Read the article** to see full details of the response

...cont'd

If the articles suggested don't resolve your query, click the **Contact Support** button.

1. You are asked to specify your product or service, and to choose a related support category

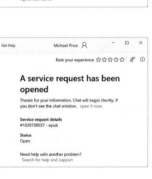

225

2. Click **Confirm** and you'll be offered the option to chat with a support agent in your web browser

3. A service request will be opened and you can discuss your query online

4. When the chat ends, you will be asked to indicate your level of satisfaction

5. Click **Submit** to complete the exchange

Hot tip

The **Get Help** app deals with Windows, Microsoft 365 and Office, Xbox, Surface and MSN, and other products. Five categories are suggested:

Billing and Account Profile questions
Manage my Subscription
Password Reset/Recovery
Technical Support
Activate my product

Beware

The support agent will resolve basic issues for free, but you may be offered an upgrade to a fee-based service for more complex issues.

Program compatibility

If you're using applications designed to run under previous versions of Windows (prior to Windows 11), you may need to enable **Compatibility** mode to let them run correctly.

 Type **Compatibility** in the Search box on the Taskbar, then select **Run programs made for previous versions of Windows**

 Click **Next** to find and fix problems with running older programs in Windows 11

Don't forget

When the test completes, select the appropriate result and take any actions suggested.

 Select a program that may have problems, then click **Try recommended settings**

④ Click **Test the program...** to see if the selected settings were successful

Windows Security

The **Windows Security** app, which is pre-installed with Windows 11, can be used to give a certain amount of protection against viruses and malicious software. To use it:

 1 Select **Settings** > **Privacy & security**

2 Click on the **Windows Security** option

3 The **Windows Security** section contains the main categories for helping to keep your Windows 11 computer safe and secure

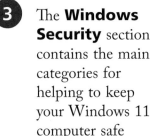

4 Click on the **Open Windows Security** button

Hot tip

Windows Security provides protection against malicious software such as viruses and spyware, so you do not have to install separate utilities.

5 The options in Step 3 can be selected in the **Windows Security** section

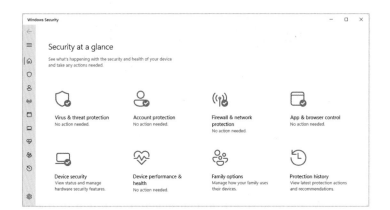

...cont'd

6 Click on the **Virus & threat protection** option to see details of the last virus checks, and the status of protection updates

7 Click on the **Quick scan** button to run a check of your system

Hot tip

Windows Security also alerts you when spyware attempts to install or run, or when apps try to change important Windows settings.

○ Virus & threat protection

Protection for your device against threats.

🔊 **Current threats**

No current threats.
Last scan: 10/6/2021 9:54 AM (quick scan)
0 threat(s) found.
Scan lasted 15 minutes 11 seconds
42526 files scanned.

[Quick scan]

Scan options

Allowed threats

Protection history

8 Once a quick scan has been completed there are options to do more scans. Check on one of the options – e.g. **Full scan** – and click on the **Scan now** button to perform the selected scan

Scan options

Run a scan from the available options on this page.

No current threats.
Last scan: 10/6/2021 9:54 AM (quick scan)
0 threat(s) found.
Scan lasted 15 minutes 11 seconds
42526 files scanned.

Allowed threats

Protection history

○ Quick scan
   Checks folders in your system where threats are commonly found.

● Full scan
   Checks all files and running programs on your hard disk. This scan could take longer than one hour.

○ Custom scan
   Choose which files and locations you want to check.

○ Microsoft Defender Offline scan
   Some malicious software can be particularly difficult to remove from your device. Microsoft Defender Offline can help find and remove them using up-to-date threat definitions. This will restart your device and will take about 15 minutes.

[Scan now]

...cont'd

 Click on the **Account protection** option to apply security settings and options for your own Microsoft account

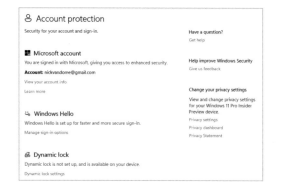

 Click on the **Device performance & health** option to view a report about the overall health of your computer

Click on the **Family options** option to apply parental controls, for children using your computer

Parental controls can be set for items such as restricting access to certain types of websites and setting time limits for using a Windows 11 device.

Windows Firewall

Within the **Windows Security** options is an important feature for using the built-in firewall, to help prevent malicious software entering your computer from the internet, via your router. To use this:

1 Open the **Windows Security** panel as shown on pages 227-229 and select **Firewall & network protection**

Firewall & network protection
No action needed.

The **Microsoft Defender Firewall** is **On** by default in Windows 11, but you can turn it **Off** if you have another firewall installed and active.

2 Select one of the options – e.g. **Private network** – to view the firewall settings for this item (by default, the firewall should be **On**)

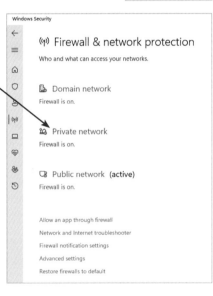

Windows Security

⁽⁽ɪ⁾⁾ Firewall & network protection
Who and what can access your networks.

Domain network
Firewall is on.

Private network
Firewall is on.

Public network (active)
Firewall is on.

Allow an app through firewall
Network and Internet troubleshooter
Firewall notification settings
Advanced settings
Restore firewalls to default

Click **Allow an app through firewall** in Step 2, to view a list of allowed apps that can communicate through **Windows Defender Firewall**. Select apps to be allowed through the firewall, as required.

3 The firewall settings for the selected item are displayed. By default, the **Microsoft Defender Firewall** should be **On**. If it is **Off**, click on it to turn the firewall **On**

Private network
Networks at home or work, where you know and trust the people and devices on the network, and where your device is set as discoverable.

Active private networks
Not connected

Microsoft Defender Firewall
Helps protect your device while on a private network.

 On

Incoming connections
Prevents incoming connections when on a private network.

☐ Blocks all incoming connections, including those in the list of allowed apps.

Windows Update

To view the status of Windows updates on your system:

 Open **Settings** > **Windows Update**

Beware

In Windows 11, **Windows Update** installs all updates automatically. At most you can defer updates for a time, but they will eventually be installed.

2 Check for updates if you wish, or select **Update history** to see which updates have been applied

3 To instruct **Windows Update** when to apply updates, select **Advanced options** > **Active hours**

Hot tip

Windows 11 updates are provided on a monthly basis for fixes, with feature updates provided annually.

 Select a **Start time** or **Finish time** and scroll to select a new time

 Click the **checkmark** icon to apply the new time (or click the **X** button to cancel any change)

...cont'd

You can apply controls to the way Windows installs updates. To make changes:

 Open **Settings** > **Windows Update**, then select **Advanced options**

- Get updates to other Microsoft products when you update Windows.
- You can choose to restart to finish applying updates, even during active hours, or over metered connections.
- See notification messages when restarts are scheduled for your system.
- Temporarily pause update installations for up to a week.
- You may be offered optional updates for features, quality or drivers.
- You can choose to pause updates for up to 5 weeks.

Don't forget

If you are using a metered connection (where charges may apply), updates won't normally be downloaded.

Recovery

If you are having problems with your PC, you can select **Recovery** from the **Additional options** section of **Advanced options**. From here, you have these options: **Reset this PC** (reinstalling Windows), **Go back** (uninstalling the latest update) or **Advanced startup** (changing your startup settings).

Symbols

A

B

C

T

U

V

W